Dog-Eared Pages Used Books presents

Handwritten: ART — THANKS FOR YOUR CONTINUOUS SUPPORT AND ENCOURAGEMENT

Ethereal Supply

The Third Annual Holiday Anthology
From Jerry's Writers Group

Handwritten: ENJOY THIS GIFT AND MY STORY ON P. 142

A Collection of Stories, Poetry and
Artwork for the 2010 Holiday Season

Handwritten signature: Bill

D1738781

Cover design by Eduardo Cerviño

TABLE OF CONTENTS

Foreword 2

Illustrations   by Linda K. Stouffer 3

Holiday Horoscope   by Jeff Smith 4

I Reach   by Isabel A. Worden-Klym 9

Pumpkin   by Eduardo Cerviño 10

Halloween   by Brian Mostoller 18

Ethereal Supply   by C.E. Mallory 19

The Christmas Tree   by Karen Cafarella 26

A Medieval Christmas   by Melanie Tighe 27

Holiday Message   by KRiel 39

An Unscheduled Stop   by C.E. Mallory 40

The Worst Christmas Wish List Item   by Jerry Cole 104

Mama   by Doris Cohen 105

A Phoenix Christmas   by Melanie Tighe 108

1968: Moonrise in Manhattan   by Lesley Sudders 109

Heavenly Star   by Richard Oppman 116

Solstice 2090   by Jerry Cole 117

A Fondness for Family by Doris Cohen 127

Reindeer   by Eduardo Cerviño 128

The New Bicycle   by Isabel A. Worden-Klym 141

The Box   by Bill Lamperes 142

Other Books by Our Authors 147

FOREWORD

Dog-Eared Pages Used Books and Jerry's Writers Group are proud to present our Third Annual Holiday Anthology. We hope this compilation enriches your holiday and everyday happiness whenever you open its pages.

We began work on this book early in 2010 and labored through the year, toiling away on our writing, editing each other's work, arguing, spiking our friends' coffee with cough syrup, deflating one another's tires out in the parking lot, and eventually uniting in agreement. The result is our best group publication to date.

This year's version is groundbreaking, inside and out. Artwork has been interspersed amongst the poems and short stories. We have stretched the holiday theme to include Halloween. Stories touch on the past, the present, possible futures, and pure flights of fancy.

Jerry's Writers Group is comprised of roughly a dozen aspiring writers with seven books published among us. Our diverse membership includes seasoned authors as well as novices. We meet every other Wednesday for the purpose of providing support to fellow members on their literary endeavors.

Newcomers are always welcome, so if you are interested in meaningful conversation, exchange of ideas, constructive criticism, and are able to leave your ego at home, please join us! Inquire at Dog-Eared Pages Used Books, 16428 North 32nd Street, Suite 111, Phoenix, Arizona, or drop us a note at melanie@dogearedpagesusedbooks.com.

Happy Holidays from Dog-Eared Pages Used Books and Jerry's Writers Group.

About the Artist

The wintry artwork in this anthology is from Linda K. Stouffer. She completes thirty paintings a month and sets them outside to cure in piles of birdseed, peanut butter and bread crumbs. After two days she retrieves any paintings marred by animals and repairs them. She touches them up employing Chinese methods and embalming fluid. The rest she burns, using the subsequent ashes to mix in with next month's paint. She manufactures her own paint and brushes, mostly from the remains of rodents and small animals. She also makes her own glue. In her spare time she studies the occult and experiments with poison.

"If an animal takes interest in my painting, then it is worthy," says Linda. "Otherwise, the painting has no heart and must be destroyed, along with all the ants. Every last one of them!" Linda has no tolerance for ants and has twice burned down her home because she thought it was infested. She served time for arson, and credits The Big House with her valuable artistic training. She has been honored by such entities as the Southwest Area Artists Association and the Recovering Violence Addiction Society.

"When they throw you in the box—that's what we call solitary confinement and they put you there for violent behavior—in the box you have days just trapped alone with your thoughts, and you go a little insane. That's when the really good inspiration comes." According to Linda, "Every artist should do a little time."

HOLIDAY HOROSCOPE
by Jeff Smith

About the Author

✎ Jeff has no idea what his real name is because he was abandoned at a post office as a newborn. He wound up being raised by animals in the wild when the postal service messed up their delivery to the adoption agency. His father was an alligator, but he identifies more with his mother, a platypus. His siblings are geese and sometimes during a business meeting he will shriek in terror, jump up on the table flapping his arms and squawk loudly at anybody wearing glasses. Given these skills, he's the de facto editor for this anthology. Says Jeff, "If anybody gets out of line in a meeting, just bite off one of their fingers. Then watch everybody quiet down and get back to work." He is politically involved, a member of the Wrath of Khan Party, and spends his spare time plotting the demise of James T. Kirk.

Capricorn (December 22 to January 19): This holiday season is your time to express yourself. Shed your years of family oppression, starting on Thanksgiving by finally telling the family matriarch you hate her cooking. Drink heavily and take chances. Borrow a hundred dollars to bet on the Detroit Lions. In December, you will not receive many gifts—far fewer than usual—meaning you'll start the New Year disappointed.

Aquarius (January 20 to February 18): You will miss Thanksgiving dinner in the hospital from a gunshot wound and have to settle for Jell-O instead. Be careful in the weeks following your release, and take advantage of the bustle of holiday traffic to evade the police who have been tailing you since they picked up your former colleague who confessed everything, including your role in the illegal enterprise, after trying to kill you. If you are smart and lucky, you'll begin the New Year in Mexico. If not, welcome to institutional life.

Pisces (February 19 to March 20): Another holiday season with the crack habit, and now you have to try to cook the turducken you bought while high. Your liver and pancreas are in serious trouble, so you might as well go on a binge, which is really the only way to tolerate your required time with the family. Detox can wait. Cheating on your mate continues to go well as you use shopping as an excuse for a quickie a few times per week. Your New Year's resolution, same as last year's and the one before that, will fail by February, again.

Aries (March 21 to April 19): What everybody has been telling you about taking the festivities too seriously is true. If you do not curb your spending on holiday displays for the yard, your monthly electric bill will cause you to file for bankruptcy. Your neighbors are weary of your garish presentation and are considering hiring the Hell's Angels to come bust you up along with defiling all your hard work. One turkey is enough for Thanksgiving; you don't need to cook seven of them to hand out chunks of meat to gawkers of your brazen property display as though it were Halloween candy. You are not actually Santa Claus and the fire department will not come to bail you out again this year. For New Year's Eve, lock yourself in a dark closet for twelve hours.

Taurus (April 20 to May 20): Your superstitious nature, which grows greater every year at this time, finally becomes strong enough to overwhelm the rest of your mind in the middle of your pumpkin pie when you start hearing voices. Yours is the sign of Robert A. Hawkins, who killed nine people at a shopping mall during the holiday season of 2007, and you hear his call to duty every night, waking up at 3:15 a.m. to load your gun. He taunts you, daring you to beat his tally. Take this opportunity to write out your thoughts in a journal. It will be worth a great deal of money to your survivors who will sell it to the tabloids. You won't make it to the end of the year.

Gemini (May 21 to June 20): Try not to give everybody food poisoning on Thanksgiving this time. You're better off getting takeout or just contributing a pie from Village Inn. The adage you've been following for years about giving a gift you personally would like to receive does not apply because most people do not share your obsession with manure, no matter how convenient it is to buy in bulk. You should have learned that after finding box upon box of soap and perfume under your Christmas tree last year. Your annual New Year's pagan ritual at the cemetery might get hit by a meteor.

Cancer (June 21 to July 22): The holidays bring out the mad scientist in you even more than the anger you harbor over your failed career. You are on the cusp of success with your flying vampire bunny and you should try using the brain from a fresh kill without the incubation period this time. Increase the electrical voltage and if it doesn't work out, it'll make for good Thanksgiving hors d'oeuvres. The local animal rights sect is onto you, but don't let them get in your way; release your new super-virus at their New Year's party. With all the online holiday shopping, your order for the magic chemicals will get overlooked.

Leo (July 23 to August 22): Serious introspection is in order. Fulfilling your dream of opening the world's first miniature driving range on Thanksgiving Day is really not a good idea. First of all, nobody pays attention to the sign you made in crayon and stapled to the top of your trailer; in fact nobody even sees it. Second, the space you have allocated in your gravel area is only big enough for one person, and that's not going to pay your rent at a dollar per one-hour session. Third, this will not become the next big craze you thought it would after your epiphany that day playing miniature golf. Actually, it is just stupid. Those tiny golf clubs you constructed out of cardboard, and tiny golf balls, canned peas painted with white-out, will not unlock millions but will disintegrate during the next rain. You'll be flat broke on Christmas and evicted on New Year's Day.

Virgo (August 23 to September 22): Your 153 cats will appreciate the turkey dinners more than you thought, and in their hunger they come after you next, so shore up your defenses and plan an escape route. Your annual holiday campaign to rescue another one every day of December is a little misguided. You are not really rescuing them, evidenced by their extreme mortality rate in your care. In fact most of them resent you, even your favorite, Liberace, although handcuffing his neck to your wrist and trying to teach him to play 'Santa Claus is Coming to Town' on the piano will earn you notoriety on YouTube. You'll have human guests around New Year's, camera crews from two documentary cable television shows, *Hoarders* and *Intervention*.

Libra (September 23 to October 22): Every holiday you wish upon a star, hoping to change your zodiac sign, but you are just a scale, not a living entity, so your wishes will never come true. Now go back to being a scale.

Scorpio (October 23 to November 21): But for the major repercussions to all human life, the holidays would be a good time for you to spend drying out. This does not refer to abstaining from alcohol consumption but rather skin moisturizing products, because you single-handedly absorb more lotion than any twenty psoriasis cases combined. This, coupled with your decision to move to the swamp, will lead to the next step in human evolution where we give up life on land and crawl back into the sea following your example. You are the future missing link. The choice is up to you! We can all die out in global warming or return to our roots. You have a lot to think about, so don't concern yourself with shopping.

Sagittarius (November 22 to December 21): Revel in this time of year, as your pickpocket skills prove most lucrative in holiday crowds, generating almost enough revenue to balance your losses at the casino. Coupled with your Santa-Claus-porn-star career, you will be on top, literally and figuratively. When you figure out how to combine these two worlds, you'll become the most hated person in the country and can lecture the college circuit, which will give you an outlet for your burgeoning arson fetish. Enjoy your Thanksgiving Hungry-Man frozen dinner; for you have work to do.

Warm Wishes

I REACH
by Isabel A. Worden-Klym

About the Author

✒ Isabel has published two books of poetry: *Old Friends and Ill-Starred Acquaintances*, and *A Shower of Leaves*. Her work has also been included in *The Second Holiday Anthology* and *The Palo Verde Pages*.

A native of Ohio, she currently lives in Glendale, Arizona, and is working on a novel.

High blue skies light the way,
now is my Christmas day.
There is no crunching snow,
nor freezing-your-toes cold.

A sniff of salty sand
connects me to this land.
Gold and vermilion,
stony chameleons
stand in the setting sun,
and then the day is done.

Purple, magenta, peach,
in somnolence I reach
for thoughts of bright colors
that Christmas dreams conjure.

PUMPKIN
by Eduardo Cerviño

About the Author

✎　Born in Havana, Cuba, Eduardo Cerviño has resided in the U.S. since 1968. He has written several novels and numerous short stories that blur the line between mystery, the paranormal and sci-fi. His most recent completed novel is entitled *In My Other Body.*

He has traveled extensively throughout the U.S., Europe, and Latin-America working as an architectural designer. Eduardo's oil paintings have been exhibited in the U.S. and abroad.

At 520 pounds the last time he was moved with the help of a crane, Mario was morbidly obese. On that day, he received his proverbial fifteen minutes of fame, when the family relocated to a small farm on the outskirts of the town and the local TV station got a whiff of the situation.

At the time, I lived on the adjacent two-acre farm, and watched the mover's van arrive. The crane lifted Mario up to the terrace, and the media crew transformed a moment of painful privacy into a grotesque entertainment news segment. Only the sound of the crane broke the silence. I felt like an intruder, but remained watching the surreal spectacle.

After the enormous blob of his body was flown up to the terrace, I walked back home, expecting never to have direct contact with him. However, I couldn't get him out of my mind. Soon thereafter he became the focal point of my social activities, and my connection to a magical world.

A large barn with a gambrel roof had been converted into a comfortable, simple home. In the former hayloft, a bedroom had been prepared to receive him. A terrace was built so the bed on wheels he occupied could be rolled out into the daylight through double doors that were left in place.

Until now, his life in the city suburbs had been confined by the four walls of a room with a patio door that opened onto a barren fenced yard. From his new, high-up perch, the expanded horizon made him feel like a child in a tree house. He decided to read again *Tarzan of the Apes.*

Mario's family had been city dwellers, not enthusiastic about rural communities, but obesity had taken a toll on their son's health. Later I would learn that Mario had come to die as he longed to live, outdoors, facing the sun.

On subsequent mornings, I saw him from afar, as his parents rolled him out to the open terrace to bask in the morning rays. Curiosity molded my behavior and I began to spy on him from my window with my binoculars. He had a pleasant face with gentle eyes, colorless lips, pale skin—lots of it—and a constant, sweet, contented smile.

I don't know when I made up my mind to visit him. Maybe it had been previously decided by both of us, as we rejoiced in the magic of the ethereal realm and chose new paths for our next lives.

* * * * *

It was difficult to decide what to take as a housewarming present; food seemed inappropriate, and a plenitude of flowers carpeted the fields following a bee-filled spring. I took my softball cap so that he could use it during his terrace escapades. I hoped the pink color was not too objectionable to him, but it was something that I thought he would find useful.

My name is Samantha Jones, I'm nineteen years old, and today, Saturday morning, I'm going to visit my neighbor.

I took a shortcut through the field where Father grew pumpkins for Halloween. I stopped a few seconds to admire the one he was grooming for the competition. It stood out above all others, and we estimated it to be over 600 pounds.

I continued on my way and noticed Mario was outside. I'd learned his name from the news program. Although I was still far away, I felt certain he was observing me.

His mother reacted to my request to visit him with the guarded courtesy of a protective parent, but she guided me upstairs.

"Mario, you have a visitor; may we come in?"

"Of course, Mom. Come in."

"Hi, Mario," I said. "I'm Samantha. I live over there." I pointed.

"I know. I've watched you come and go to see that pumpkin. Do you want to hear something funny, Samantha?"

"I guess so; what is it?"

"Tell her, Mom. Tell her my nickname."

She hesitated, then turned to me and said, "Pumpkin."

Mario was the first to laugh, a genuine, enjoyable, ponderous laugh that shook the bed and was impossible not to join in.

"Please sit if you want," he said, and I accepted after a quick look around the terrace.

Maria, his mother, was still measuring me. "What can I offer you, Samantha?"

There was a cup by Mario's side, close to his hand.

"Whatever he's having would be fine."

"Coffee, black, no sugar?" she questioned and I nodded.

"I'll be back. Feel at home, please," said Maria.

By the time she returned, Mario and I had found various themes of mutual interest. Convinced I was not motivated by insensitive curiosity, she relaxed.

As we talked, I learned of his insatiable curiosity about school, which he could not attend. He was educated with the help of home tutors. His vocabulary was eloquent, his prose lyrical at times. I asked if he liked poetry. He pointed to still-unpacked boxes strewn around the room. "My books: novels, poetry, and history." He pulled a book from under the pillows and handed it over. "*Tales of the Alhambra*, by Washington Irving, 1851 edition. Have you read it?" he asked.

"No. What is it about?" I responded. He explained about the book and its connection to a poem written by Alexander Pushkin and an opera by Rimsky-Korsakov.

"Take it with you. I just finished it for a third time. Reading is my way to travel. I do not get around much, as you might imagine."

This was the first of many visits. Mario's body, constrained as it was, could not hold his imagination in place. When fall turned the corner, we were the best of friends. He had opened my mind to the world, set my soul in flight, and I was in love—but not with him.

* * * * *

My friends and I met regularly in the college library. We represented a cross-section of the student body and were coordinating the design of the school float for the Halloween parade. For six weeks we had been tossing around ideas and had developed a preliminary concept, selected the music for the school band, and the costumes for the float occupants.

"We will need lots of your father's pumpkins for the float. I hope he gives us a decent price and we don't have to buy them at the supermarket," said Francis. "Would you talk to him about that, Samantha?" He was our treasurer in charge of the limited budget, and the star of the track team. He had an olive complexion, black eyes and hair, and his square jaw stood six feet above the ground.

He is six seven at least. I would have to stand on my toes, if I ever get to kiss him, I thought.

Francis neither encouraged nor discouraged my obvious infatuation with him. However, he glanced and smiled at me more often than he did the other girls. The exception was Roselyn. I was jealous of her, but not sure of his intentions toward the long-legged brunette with a resemblance to Angelina, the well-known movie star.

One afternoon we got a tip about the competing school's float; it was similar to ours, but was already under construction.

"Everybody will say we copied them. You have to come up with a more unique idea," said the drama coach, sending our brains into a spin.

The same afternoon I visited Mario. He commented about how big my father's pumpkin was. "It's bigger than me," he said and laughed. "I've given it a name: from now on she is Alice." We laughed.

"It's true, Alice looks a lot bigger," I said. No sooner had I said it than an idea popped into my mind.

"Mario, would you like to go to the parade?" I asked and his laughter stopped.

"Are you joking with me?"

"Not at all. Would you like to go?" No answer, but a long serious stare into my eyes.

"I'm sorry," I said. "I did not think it through."

An awkward minute later, Mario spoke. "I would. I would like to go to the parade, Samantha."

* * * * *

The concept was extreme and the team loved it. Ideas flowed like chocolate syrup, and the next day I called Mario to ask permission for the team to visit him. His mother was shocked at first, while his father was outright angry.

"Do they want to parade my son as a circus freak? Don't they have enough excitement with the cheerleaders?" he yelled.

"Calm down, please; you have been drinking too much," said Maria.

Then I heard Mario's voice over the phone, "Daaad! It's about time."

"About time for what, son?" said his father, still yelling.

"Not to hide me anymore, Dad. Descartes once said, 'I think, therefore I am.' Despite all you see, Dad, I am a person. I'm willing to go if they are willing to take me."

"What does a cart have to do with this?"

"Never mind, Dad. I'm sorry if I shame you. Let them come here and talk."

Maria came back on the line. "Samantha, you are welcome anytime."

From that moment on, the project moved fast. I came every day to keep Mario in the loop. Sometimes others came with me. We laughed and planned every detail, including life insurance, in case the crane dropped him.

One day I came too early and Maria asked me to come back later. I asked why, and she said, "We are giving him a bath." I had never thought about it and felt sort of repulsed by the images that flooded my mind.

"I'm sorry about that," I said. "I mean, I'll be back."

I left, walking a little faster than usual. I looked back at the house and caught Maria's facial expression. It was deep and sad, as if she had taken a peek inside my head.

* * * * *

Mario became anxious as the day approached. He obsessed over details. "When alone, I watch the giant pumpkin. I can feel it growing proud like a sumo wrestler," he told me once. I ignored the remark, but it was true that the pumpkin was increasing its girth remarkably fast. My father had noticed it.

Halloween morning, the float was below his terrace; it depicted a vine packed with real pumpkins crawling up a hill full of girls in animal costumes: rabbits and birds. Atop the hill was Mario's place. The crane flew him from his bed to the float, where he sat dressed in a costume resembling the giant pumpkin; his head represented the stem.

As we moved away from the farm, Mario looked at the pumpkin. "Bye, my friend. I will tell you all about it when I return. I know how it feels to be stuck."

It was a fun afternoon. The band walked in front. The girls on the float exchanged quips with Mario, and his cleverness gave them a harder time that they expected. People applauded; there was no pity, no cruel outburst from the crowd, and Mario was now a famous town resident.

Back at the farm, the crane had carried Alice onto a trailer to be moved to the fairgrounds. The trailer stood by the side of the house below Mario's terrace. The sun was reclining at the edge of the evening when Mario was lifted up.

"Would you raise me as high as you can before taking me to my bed, please, and then shut off the engine and let me rest a few minutes in silence," requested Mario.

* * * * *

"How did you feel up there?" I asked him later.

"I imagined I was a bird. It was such a sweet vision. I flew to the top of the big pumpkin and told her what I did today; you know, we commiserated, pumpkin to pumpkin."

Almost everyone had left. I was alone with Mario on the terrace, quietly releasing the lingering euphoria. We heard voices and I went to see. It was Francis and Roselyn.

"It was nice to win first place, and we did not spend the entire budget," said Roselyn, unaware their voices carried up to us. They sat at the edge of the trailer, with their backs toward Alice.

"We were lucky that Samantha convinced that freak to go along for the ride. We couldn't lose," said Francis.

"She is so naive. You're right—she thinks you are in love with her," she said.

"It saved us almost four hundred dollars on the cost of the pumpkins."

"Poor thing; she should look in the mirror. In a few more years, she will be as fat as he is. My gosh, Samantha is at least fifty pounds overweight," said Roselyn.

"The two of them can compete with this monster, fat pumpkin," he added.

Tears made my eyes glossy. I turned my face towards Mario. His eyes were aflame with anger; his clenched fists made his knuckles yellow, and he shook on his bed, as he attempted to stand up.

I heard a noise below and looked down. Alice was rocking the trailer bed. Francis and Roselyn turned around to look at the pumpkin, and saw me.

Surprised, they did not move. As Alice barreled down on them, they jumped to the ground, but it was too late. Alice vaulted from her bed, and landed on top of them. I gasped, horrified.

I had heard my father estimate Alice's weight at 1400 pounds.

HALLOWEEN
by Brian Mostoller

This is a pumpkin place,
of snarled vines
and whisper shapes
from wind
in dusk.
A full-decked moon hovers,
a startled crow flutters feathers
then drifts over a plain
frosting
resting
as the night folds over.

Rolling my bicycle back and forth
beneath me
I hear the tires crunch leaves
and wonder from what tree they came.
My life,
dusk,
and the enfolding.

ETHEREAL SUPPLY
by C.E. Mallory

About the Author

✍ Composer/author C.E. (Chuck) Mallory is a late bloomer. After successful careers as a musician, arranger/composer-conductor and businessman, he is now emergent on the literary horizon where he believes his star is destined to rise. Chuck has completed the first two movements of a symphony for large orchestra and ninety-five percent of a contemporary oratorio that's the product of many years of soul searching, song writing and composing. He says the novel stewing in his brain will have to wait until those two projects are totally finished.

After spending many years in southern California, Chuck moved to and has resided in Phoenix, Arizona for the past six years. He has two grown children and describes himself as a "happy recluse."

It has been said that "Truth is stranger than fiction." This is a true story taken from his new book, *Beans & Rice and Jesus Christ*, coming soon to major book stores near you.

Los Angeles, California. Summer, 1977

Percy Harris was more than a little upset with himself. He was quite upset. Somehow, he had run out of money—almost flat out. That was no real disaster in and of itself, but the timing was all wrong. His military retirement check would arrive before the third of January, but this was December 23rd, and being broke at Christmas meant disappointing somebody. He realized he'd overspent on gifts and hadn't left enough for the big dinner. If he didn't get some cash in a hurry, he wasn't going to be able to serve his usual lavish holiday banquet. Downgrading to salami sandwiches and soda pop was not an acceptable option. When he checked his emergency cash stash, his mood went from glum to glummer. It was the glummest he'd been in a long time.

"This will never do," he chided himself.

Young and single, he liked to cook and entertain. The ex-army sergeant especially enjoyed being able to feed some of the one-parent kids in his apartment building who were sure to drop by. The children and their single parents, usually just a mother, needed and appreciated his frequent largesse. They knew his door was ever open and his table always set. He was warm-hearted and open-handed to a fault, and everyone had a perpetual welcome at Percy's. Whatever the problem of the moment, his sympathetic ear was sure to be available and he was unfailingly ready to help. Whether it was an ice cream cone on a blistering summer day, a bowl of hot soup on a chilly autumn evening, or an inexpensive toy at Christmas, he was known to give it. The entire apartment building knew and loved the young retiree, especially the children. For a man who had no children, Percy Harris had bought an awful lot of school supplies.

At forty-two, he'd already been retired from the military a little over five years, and had lived in his comfortable second floor unit since coming to Los Angeles after his military severance. His always high spirits made him always welcome, and his popularity rating was somewhere above the Easter Bunny's and only slightly less than Santa Claus'. In short, everyone loved him and he returned the favor.

"Maybe I can borrow a few dollars from George," he mused. George Lincoln was an old friend who had served with him on his second tour of duty in Viet Nam. He picked up the phone, called George, and immediately got loan approval from his old army buddy.

"I'm off from work at three," George said. "I'll be at your place by four. We can stroll over to the Boys Market. I need to pick up the rest of the grocery list my wife gave me. I'll cash my paycheck and loan you whatever you need."

"Great, George. Thanks! I knew I could count on you."

"Now Percy, haven't we always counted on each other? Remember that last firefight we had with the Viet Cong? Do you think I could say no to a man who was wounded worse than I and still hoisted me on his back and ran us both to safety?

"Trying to sprint with you over my shoulder isn't what I remember, George. What *I* remember most is all that cussin' you were doing! In all my years as an army sergeant, I've never heard anybody cuss like that. You mother-F'd 'em from

Amazing Grace to *How Sweet the Sound!!* As I recall, both you and your M-16 were doing some very serious cussin'!"

"I don't know if they understood good old-fashioned English profanity, but I know they understood AK-47 and M-16!"

"Enough war stories! I'll see you at four?"

"Four it is, my man!"

The television remote had fallen to the floor and Percy was dozing in his recliner when the doorbell snatched him back to reality at 3:55 p.m. He and George hugged like long lost brothers; as only men who've narrowly escaped death together can, they truly appreciated seeing each other, alive, whole, and well.

By four, they had made the short walk across the rough parking lot between Percy's apartment building and the Boys Supermarket. The parking lot was crowded, and the busy market teemed with holiday shoppers who threatened to burst it at the seams. George's wife had given him a fairly long list to complete, so between that list and the crowd, they weren't exactly going to be in and out. It was forty-five minutes before they made it to the checkout line.

The male shopper ahead of George kept up a flirtatious patter with the big-bosomed female cashier as she rang up his purchases. George and Percy looked knowingly at each other, winked and sighed, mentally agreeing that his hit-on-the-cashier technique was weak. Predictably, she declined to give him her phone number. Percy helped George empty his grocery cart onto the conveyor. That's when it happened.

The first thing Percy noticed was the strange silence. It wasn't really eerie, and there was nothing frightening about it. Still, it was somehow disconcertingly odd. In the midst of the teeming supermarket, his hearing seemed to have faded away. He wasn't sure if he heard, or felt, his own heart beat. He knew he could still hear, but all he heard was a thunderously unnatural silence. He could see people talking, their lips moving soundlessly. The market's background music was gone, now as silent as their intercom. The usually noisy cash registers were operating silently. It was beyond strange; this ultra silent world.

Percy looked around him. Out of the corner of his eye, some movement caught his attention. It was then that he saw the first bill. Fluttering in the air like a feather, the five dollar bill fell slowly to the floor in front of him. Before it landed, he saw three other bills in the air, floating slowly down like snowflakes. He looked up toward the ceiling, then all around him. The air was filled with money! It was snowing currency—out of nowhere! Eyes wide, mouth agape, Percy Harris watched in utter disbelief for almost a minute as money drifted slowly to the floor all around him.

Then, it was over as suddenly as it began. He heard the canned Christmas music once more as the last bill fluttered to the ground. When he looked down, the money seemed to have landed all around him, no one else. It was all in his immediate vicinity, even on the tops of his shoes. There were ones, fives, a couple of tens, even a twenty. He bent over and picked up every bill, pocketing them one by one. No one seemed to notice. The lady behind him in line seemed to be oblivious to what had happened, or what he was doing as he collected the money.

Likewise, both George and the checkout clerk seemed equally oblivious. Timorously, Percy turned to the lady in the checkout line behind him and asked her, "Did you see all that money?"

"What money?" she said.

"All that money floating in the air! You had to see it—didn't you?"

She said absolutely nothing, but the look she gave him said, "I'm talking to a certified nut!"

George was still endorsing his paycheck when Percy asked the cashier, "Have you ever seen anything like that before? Wasn't that amazing?"

"What?" she asked innocently.

"Why, the money! Dollars falling to the floor out of thin air! Didn't you see it? Didn't you see the money?"

"Sorry. I didn't see any money. Did you?" She gave George his change and pushed the last of his groceries down the counter toward the bag boy who was loading George's shopping cart.

George had parked in the store's lot before going into Percy's building, so they took the groceries directly to his car. The bags filled both the trunk and the rear seat.

"Tell me, George," Percy asked, "did you notice anything at all strange while we were checking out?"

"No, not particularly. I noticed that that lovelorn Lothario in front of us couldn't pick up a woman if he was in a women's prison with a satchel full of pardons!"

"You didn't see any money on the ground—or in the air?"

"Money on the ground? Or in the air? You're kidding me, right?" He burst into laughter, slapping his thigh. "Percy, you are such a card! By the way, how much did you need from me?" He was reaching for his wallet.

Percy felt the wad of bills in the front pocket of his Levi jeans. It was a comforting bulge. He didn't know how much he had, but he felt certain that it was more than enough to cover a big Christmas dinner.

"Thank you, George," he said. "You know I really appreciate having a friend like you, and your being willing to help me out. Just seeing you is a blessing; right now, I don't need anything more. If I should, I'll let you know."

"Are you sure? It's not a problem, you know!"

"I'm positive. Thanks."

"Okay. Call me any time."

"Tell the wife and kids I said Merry Christmas!"

"I'll do that, and she told me to be sure to tell you that you are both invited and expected for dinner at our place on New Year's Day. All right?"

"I will be there. I promise. That honey-glazed ham Marie fixed last New Year was unforgettable!"

As George eased out of the parking lot and merged with the busy La Brea Avenue traffic, Percy felt the bills in his pants pocket once again. This time, he pulled them out and counted. Had he borrowed money from George, he'd have had to repay it. Integrity and honor required that. But he saw no way to give back this mysterious bounty from the universe which had materialized out of thin air and fallen at his feet, unseen by anyone, and witnessed only by God's profound silence. He still couldn't believe it. If he hadn't been holding the cash, he wouldn't have.

He counted 110 dollars.

"I have to remember the yams and the cranberry sauce," he said to himself as he headed back into the supermarket.

The holidays are here!

THE CHRISTMAS TREE
by Karen Cafarella

We had a fake Christmas tree when I was a child. It was six feet tall and to me it was the most beautiful tree in all the world. Each year when Dad brought it down from the attic and started unpacking its box, I couldn't wait to help put it up. I really should say put it *together*. Once the "trunk" was assembled we would affix the branches. The tips of their wire inserts were color coded to match spots on the trunk. A real tree never occurred to me.

Years later, after I married, we decided a real tree was preferable. Since the kids had not experienced snow growing up in Phoenix, we traveled north together as a family. We figured they could play in the snow a while, and we would find our tree. We obtained a permit to cut one down, and when we arrived the forest was blanketed in snow.

It was so scenic, so tranquil. The ground was covered and snow clumped on the branches of all the trees. The kids immediately jumped out to scamper around and play in it. When they had enough we started our hunt. All the trees looked beautiful and it was hard to pick one.

We heard our oldest shout, "This is it!" We gathered to look at it and saw how perfect it was: deep green, strong and symmetrical. Before we started chopping we attempted to gauge it, because it was standing next to some very tall others. Our initial perception of its height was way off, and we realized it was a rather tall tree itself. We explained perspective to our son, and how the tree appears shorter when amongst its tall brethren. We had to devise a way to assess height without a measuring tape, so we had my husband stand next to each tree, as he was the tallest at the time, and judged each one from there.

We finally found a tree we all loved, chopped it down and home we went. We loved the smell, and even the mess! That Christmas was a little extra special to us all.

A MEDIEVAL CHRISTMAS
by Melanie Tighe

About the Author

✎ Melanie Tighe owns Dog-Eared Pages Used Books and has just completed her first novel, *The Minstrel's Tale*. Written for children ages ten and older, the book combines real history with fun fairy tales. We have all read about or watched movies of Christmas celebrations of nineteenth century England, but hundreds of years before that, holiday traditions were drastically different. Since her mind was in the fourteenth century she thought it would be fun to take a peek at the holiday customs of that era in Europe.

Four more days! was my first thought as I threw back the quilt on my bed and wiped the sleepy grit from my eyes. I already knew what I would do if chosen; in fact I had been planning it since last Childermass. Before that we had much work to do, for today was Adam and Eve Day and many of the townsfolk would be pouring into our tavern for their evening meals.

Mama kept my younger brother Jonathan and I so busy that we missed out on hanging apples on the large fir tree at the church next to our inn. I did not so much regret missing decorating the tree; it was the crisp taste of the juicy, late harvest apples I craved.

Mama made a gigantic pot of wassail from ale, honey and spices, and the sweet smell of cinnamon filled every corner of the inn. Jonathan's chore was to stir the wassail, keeping it hot but not bubbling. I envied him, for he was wiping sweat from his face while I was chilled to the bone from carting in firewood, caring for guests' horses and keeping the wash stand, just outside the door, filled with fresh water. Each time I had to break through the crust of ice formed over the bucket before I could refill the pitcher and bowl.

Following Mama's recipe our serving girls, Janessa and Claudine, spent the morning baking up batches of frumenty in little bowls filled with porridge and dried fruit spiced with cloves and nutmeg. It had spent the day cooling. Now Mama and the girls scurried to serve both the frumenty and mince pies to our guests all the while keeping their tankards filled.

Many of the townsfolk waited at our tavern, eating and drinking until the bells rang out signaling the beginning of the Angels Mass held at midnight. Then they all charged out at once, leaving us in peace. Janessa and Claudine hurried after them while I prayed Mama would not insist we attend the Mass, drawing a relieved breath when she sighed and fell into a chair. I could tell she was exhausted. Her coppery hair fell in curled wisps from her tight braid and lay plastered by sweat against her face.

"They'll be back soon," she said blowing a stray hair out of her eye. "We've still much to do."

I plunked into a chair beside her, "We will get it done, Mama; rest a while."

Jonathan brought us each a mug of wassail and settled onto the floor between us. We sipped our drinks in silence until Matthew lumbered in. His gigantic frame filled the door and a powdery snow covered his wide shoulders. "We have enough wood split to last through Twelfth Night," he announced before shrugging off his cloak.

"Rest a while, Matthew," Mama told him. He had been in Mama's service since before I was born and we all knew Matthew would work til he collapsed if he thought it would please Mama. "Jonathan–"

Before she could finish, my brother bounced up, filled a mug with hot wassail and delivered it to Matthew. "Much thanks, Master Jonathan."

If Papa were here, we would have been at Mass. Our many servants would have handled the guests at our former inn while Mama spent the morning making sure Jonathan and I were presentable enough to attend the church service. We used to go to the Christmas Mass with King Richard at St. Paul's Cathedral in London where the monks sang quiet hymns and the Archbishop presided over the Mass.

In this smaller town, the church was nowhere near the size of the great cathedral and instead of monks chanting, rowdy carolers were pitched out of the church for singing during

Mass. I watched from the window as they stood shivering in separate little clusters, each group heartily bellowing a different song.

"Mama, they all look so cold," I said.

"Go ahead, Amos," she sighed.

I filled as many mugs as I could carry and flung open the door. The merry carolers flocked to me as hens at feeding time and I handed out the warm drinks, ducking back inside for more. They expressed their gratitude by singing even louder, but at least for the moment they were all singing the same tune.

We did not have many travelers at this time of year, but the few who stayed the night would be returning from Mass soon and would more than likely want to go right to sleep, for at dawn the Shepherd's Mass would begin.

I knew Mama would insist we attend the morning Mass. Skipping one service, although frowned upon, could be forgiven, while missing two would not. I am uncertain what happens if you miss too many, but I have heard rumors of souls burning in Satan's fires for all eternity for lesser offenses. I believe Mama was more concerned with other rumors. Rumors any woman, without a husband near to support her and a successful inn, might fear. Rumors of witchcraft.

She had explained how tiny transgressions could be blown into evidence of the evil crime and how we would have to be on guard until Papa returned. Mama spoke as if from experience, but she was no more a witch than the Pope. When I asked her about it, she only shook her head and would speak no more of it.

Jonathan and I went to bed for the few hours before dawn. Mama and Matthew stayed up awaiting the return of our guests and I could hear them in the kitchen readying the food to break our fast after we returned from the church.

Three more days! I thought as the priest droned on. There was only one other boy who might beat me out, but by now many people in the town knew me and I was confident I had a better chance than Thomas Raville since he had already won last year. Besides, if I could not win, I hoped it was Tom. He and I had been friends since we moved here and I knew if he won, it would still be a day to remember forever.

I had trouble keeping my eyes open. Jonathan did not even try so I elbowed him and he awoke with a start, "Wha?"

"Shh!" I hissed.

Mama seemed to be sleeping with her eyes open. As I watched her, she barely even blinked, her gaze focused on the priest. I tried to imitate her and found the priest becoming hazy and blurry as if hidden by a cloud. The harder I stared the fuzzier he became, until I blinked and he snapped into sharp focus for a moment. I could also make the priest grow taller and thinner if I turned my head just so and squinted hard until the lights from the candles almost seemed to sprout from his head. The only thing I could not do was make him end the service and I groaned as I realized later today the Mass of the Divine Word would be held.

I do not remember the services at the cathedral in London lulling me to sleep as this one did. I guess when you are giving Mass for the King, it would not do to put the King to sleep. I missed the singing monks who broke up the tiresome sermons.

Of the twelve days of Christmas, I found Christmas Day to be the most boring. All day we were either at church or working hard for the customers visiting our inn between services.

The next morning was St. Stephen's Day which left only two more days until Childermass. I found these services more interesting as mummers played out different parts in the story of Christ and Matthew was given the part of the evil King Herod.

The priests frowned as we all laughed, for though he tried to look mean and villainous, everyone knew him to be a kind soul. As he struggled to appear wicked, he succeeded only in looking as if he needed to relieve himself as he ordered the death of all the innocent children in the land.

After the service, the priests opened the alms box and handed out coins to the poor peasants who lined the steps into the church.

Mummers played for the next two days throughout the town. The men dressed in the clothing of women and women dressed as men. Each play featured a different King Herod; even Tom's father, Master Raville, tried his hand at it. He at least looked the part of a king for, aside from the mayor, he was the wealthiest merchant in Poitiers. Like Matthew, everyone knew him to be a gentle man and he too earned laughter from us all. The best Herod was Ferrand the smithy, his cold, dark eyes and black hair lending him the very face of evil. When he glowered over us all, we had no doubt he could order the death of all the children. However, the next part he played, as the wife of the innkeeper who turned Joseph and Mary away, made us howl with laughter since his dress was too short and his hairy legs stuck out the bottom.

Afterwards, the men would stop at our tavern and order mug after mug of ale until they were stumbling around in their skirts and tripping over their hems. More than one fell face down and Matthew would haul them out, leaving them sitting along side the inn until they sobered enough to make it home.

A ring of light circled the three-quarter moon and whispers of snow spread. I was not worried; I had already planned for that possibility and almost favored snow to the plan I had devised for a clear day.

I was up before dawn, not wanting to miss a moment of Childermass. I readied myself in haste and spent endless moments hurrying Mama and Jonathan along. It seemed they moved with unnatural slowness this morning and I could not tell if they were trying to vex me or not. The sky was clear so I decided to keep my snow plan secret and perhaps pass it along to Jonathan two years hence, when he would be of age.

The church was already filled when we arrived and I searched the faces for Tom. We had a pact that no matter who won, the other would be second in command. I found him standing against the wall, whispering with his younger sister, teasing her no doubt, as that was his favorite pastime.

I squeezed past a bevy of prattling, plump goodwives and wove through the clusters of chattering parishioners making my way to Tom's side. As ever, Jonathan trailed behind me. "Merry day," I greeted him. Although at fourteen summers, he was a year older than me, I stood as tall as he.

"By the bones of Judas! I was beginning to wonder if you would make it," he scolded.

"Well, I am here now. When do you think they'll choose?"

"Any moment—look, there is Father Paul now," he pointed to the altar where the youngest priest swept up to the dais, his scarlet robes brushing the flagstone floor in his wake.

"Here it comes!" Tom whispered.

Father Paul seemed to take wicked delight in stretching out the time. His clear voice boomed through the church, and several times I caught him glancing at Tom and me as he delivered his sermon about the sin of pride.

After what seemed like forever, he dropped his voice to almost a whisper. "Today, in remembrance of the Holy Innocents, we celebrate by appointing an innocent," chuckles broke out throughout the church and even Father Paul smirked at the term, "boy to the role of Bishop of Poitiers."

"This year," he continued, "the wise brothers of the church have selected…" he paused; we waited and I could not help but think, *this must be the only time of year when the priests could hold the attention of every child in town, and they intended to make it last.*

"Amos Questerly!"

I was not sure I really heard my name or just wished it so, until Tom clapped me on the back shouting, "Bishop Questerly, we await your command!"

A path opened before me and I made my way to the dais to take over control of the town of Poitiers until sunset.

Even I knew it was a mad custom to allow a child to reign over the town, but I intended to take full advantage, for the tradition that followed at sundown was not at all to my liking and if I was forced to participate in that one, I might as well enjoy this one while it lasted. "Thomas Raville, I shall require your services," I shouted.

Tom bounded up beside me, the grin stretched across his face, I had not given him so much as a hint as to my plans and I was gratified by his eager faith in my ability to make this a Childermass that would be talked about for generations.

"Master Raville, Mayor Perry, we will have need of your fastest horses and your coaches for the day," I announced.

Murmurs spread through the congregated crowd. Master Raville was the first to respond, "At your disposal, sir!" he answered with a deep bow and a playful grin.

The Mayor, alarm clear on his face, asked, "What are your intentions, Bishop Questerly?"

This was the moment I had been waiting for; I took a deep breath, "Over the past year, I have noticed the drivers of these particular coaches race through town causing people to jump out of their way." I paused as I heard whispers of agreement pass through the church. Everyone knew to get out of the way when Master Raville's coach flew through the streets, whereas the Mayor's more sedate pace drew no alarm. But for my plan I needed two fast carriages and these were the fastest in town.

"Bishop Questerly," the Mayor began, "I concede Master Raville's speeds are at times dangerous, but my own, I assure you–"

Tom cut him off, "Mayor, are you denying our Bishop the use of your coach?"

"No, no, of course not, it is just that–"

Tom interrupted again. I was glad he was by my side. I do not know if I could have handled the Mayor so well. "Then bring the coaches to the market cross within the hour!" he ordered.

Everyone looked up to me and I nodded gravely as I had watched the priests do when answering a question.

Tom and I filed out of the church behind everyone else. "What in Christendom are you up to, Questerly?" he asked when we were alone.

"Racing!" I answered.

"Racing?"

"Like they did in Rome, in the old days."

"Here?" he asked.

I nodded. "How fast do you think we can get them to go?" I asked.

He shrugged, "Depends on who is driving I guess."

"We are!"

He punched me in the shoulder, "By the bones of Judas! You are a wily one!"

"We're really going to earn tonight's reckoning," I warned.

He laughed, "I make it a point to earn mine every year!"

A mob had gathered at the market cross and parents exchanged worried glances as their children pushed through to the front, their bubbling eagerness clear as they wondered what I had in store for them.

Raville's black coach pulled up, glistening in the morning sun. His matched team of black mares pawed at the ground, impatience clear in their eyes, they blew foggy streams of hot breath into the cold air.

The Mayor's larger crimson coach followed and his pair of dappled grays at once caught the scent of excitement in the air. Their ears flicked forward then lay back flat against their heads as they tried to settle on whether to be frightened or delighted.

Tom and I moved through the crowd to the carriages. I turned and faced the townsfolk, intentionally avoiding Mama's glare as I announced, "Today we will learn which of these teams is the fastest. From the east gate," I pointed and swept my arm in an arc over my head, "to the west gate!" A buzz of excitement waved through the crowd and shouted wagers soon took over.

"Who will drive?" a voice called out.

"Tom Raville will drive his father's coach, and I will drive the Mayor's!"

Master Raville laughed aloud, but the Mayor looked anxious. I suffered a moment of regret as I realized he had more than likely voted for me out of trust, which I was now betraying, but I shook it off as I thought he too was once young enough to have done something just as outrageous, and I knew in time I could earn back his trust.

Both Tom's mama and mine shoved their way toward us. "Amos, I do not think this is wise. Let the drivers drive the coaches," Mama said.

I shook my head, "We will be fine Mama. I have waited all year for this. Wager a penny on my team, would you?"

She said not a word about the wager. Instead she grabbed my ear and squeezed. "You had better be careful," she ordered, "I want none of your blood spilled here this day." I could hear Tom getting similar warnings from his own mother as I nodded my understanding.

Our mothers melted back into the crowd and we climbed aboard the two coaches. The grays looked even bigger from up here and I wondered nervously for a moment if my mother was right.

I shrugged off my fear and turned the team toward the east gate. Tom and I both took our time, turning the teams and lining them up for the start. Tom nodded he was ready.

I shouted, "Off!" and smacked the heavy reins down. My coach lurched as the horses dug their hooves into the frozen dirt. The wheels creaked faster and faster as I whipped the reins up and down shouting, "Yup! Yup!" The horses seemed to understand, for out of the corner of my eye, I saw the black blur of Tom's team falling back bit-by-bit. Shouts rose to greet us as we roared toward the market cross, reaching a thunderous level for an instant and then fading as we sped by.

A black shape inched by and I realized Tom had pulled slightly ahead. I stood on the platform and thrashed the leather straps. I felt as if I were flying, the icy wind blowing past until my face burned and then grew numb. Tom and I were side by side and I risked a glance over to see a giant smile frozen on his face. I lashed the reigns again, shouted "Yup!" and pulled ahead just in time to see the open west gate.

The gate was only wide enough for one carriage to pass through. One of us would have to pull ahead by more than the length of the coach. I whooped up, pumped the reigns again, and saw Tom doing the same. We were still too close, and the gate was looming ahead.

I knew without looking that all of the townsfolk were running behind us. Tom pulled ahead by a bit, and I knew I would have to fall back or we would crash. I let up on the reins but the grays were now into the spirit of the race and sped on. I gathered the reins and, leaning back with all my might, tried to bring the team under control. Tom raced ahead through the gate, while my team veered at the last second, hugging tight against the wall, the wheels scraping along the stone, before settling to a stop.

My legs trembled as I stood on the halted coach, the reins still wound tight in my fists and the sides of the horses heaving as great gusts of mist streamed from their flared nostrils. I turned the team in time to watch Tom's victorious re-entry into town, the blacks prancing, their tales and heads held high as if they knew they were champions.

We stood on our coaches grinning at each other as the rest of the town caught up. Cheers followed and coin changed hands as we walked the teams back to the market crossing.

I raised my arms signaling for quiet and once I had their attention ordered the Mayor and Master Raville to give every child a ride in the coaches. The usual Childermass traditions followed, such as extra servings of frumenty, honey cakes and wassail for all children, with no chores for the entire day.

The children cheered and the parents groaned as they did every year. I climbed down from the coach. Tom and I met up and he followed me to the inn where I knew, contrary to my own commands, I would help Mama for the rest of the day.

"That was something! I have never gone so fast in my life!" Tom shouted.

"Yes," I agreed with a long sigh of contentment. Although I had not won the race, I had won the day; they would not forget this Childermass for years and Jonathan would have a lot to live up to.

No sooner had the last rays of the sun dipped below the wall, Mama got even. For the memory of Holy Innocents Day was to remind us of the killing of all the children. By custom, we were not killed, but beaten by our parents. Mama wailed on my backside while barely tapping Jonathan's. Of course, I was big enough now that it did not really hurt and I smiled to myself remembering the wind whipping past as I flew through the town.

Life settled back down for the remaining days of Christmas and although we endured the daily Mass, I welcomed Twelfth Night, for I had saved a little coin and bought Mama a present. She had not received a gift since before Papa had been arrested and she worked so very hard each day.

I did not dare tell Jonathan about it until just before we presented it to her, for he could not keep anything secret for more than a moment. That evening, Mama gave a box to each of us and we opened them to find new shirts along with gingered sweets inside. We thanked her and I handed her the small box from behind my back.

"What is this?" she asked.

"A gift for you," Jonathan and I answered together.

Tears spilled from her eyes, and I felt a growing lump in my throat. "Do not cry, Mama," I said.

She wiped away the tears, and laughed as she told us they were happy tears. She opened the box and pulled out the strands of colored ribbons I had stuffed inside.

"Thank you, my good boys," she cried as she hugged us to her.

Although we still missed Papa, it was a memorable time for all of us and I knew we would make it until Papa returned.

HOLIDAY MESSAGE
by KRiel

My fellows and I,
all with jolly visage,
traversed the many and winding roads
from recluse to fine neighbor,
up one pathway and down another,
with our cups of wassail,
and friendly cheer,
a caroling, we did go,
to share the spirit of the season
with all and sundry folk,
to perchance laugh and commune
on what is happening here,
and to wish all's well
and happiness in the coming new year.

But,
I ask you,
in this the year of
our Lord, two thousand ten,
why don't I just
say it this way–

My friends and I,
quite drunk on the
holiday season
and, of course, some beer,
went wandering our neighborhood,
laughing, singing and
bringing our message to all we met;
and here is our cheer
To all our friends, everywhere–
May love's wealth
fill your hearts
and bring you gifts of joy, health
and the promise of
Happy Holidays and a great New Year!

AN UNSCHEDULED STOP
by C.E. Mallory

Note from the Author

✒ In 2008 I wrote a short holiday story entitled *Christmas Snitchery*. It presented a non-traditional picture of Santa Claus. That story was followed a year later by *Angelic Witchery*, which opened an even larger window into the lives of Santa and his companions. Both stories can be read in 2009's *The Second Annual Holiday Anthology* by Jerry's Writers Group, available online and at Dog-Eared Pages Used Books in Phoenix, Arizona. The 2009 edition features spellbinding offerings from authors Karen Cafarella, Eduardo Cerviño, W. Jerald Cole, Brian Mostoller, Lesley Sudders, Isabel A. Worden-Klym, and Melanie Tighe. Enjoyable though I hope my earlier installments may be, they are not in any way a necessary prologue to the understanding and enjoyment of this sequel.

Santa Claus looked at his near naked body in the full length mirror and grinned. "Nick, my man," he congratulated himself, "you are back—all the way back!"

He struck a classic body builder's pose and flexed his biceps and his pectorals. Sweat glistened on his arms and ran down his chest as he half turned to get a better look at the new and much-improved physique. He'd never had washboard abs before.

"Just call me Adonis," he said to himself, remembering the Greek God. He walked around his treadmill and over to the weight bench where he began to add several plates to the bar. He wanted to bench press 275 pounds before this workout ended. He caught another glimpse of himself in the mirror as he lay down on the bench and prepared to hoist the weight. Two years earlier when he began his recovery, he couldn't have lifted the bar, much less any additional weight.

"Nick," he said to himself, "you have come a long way in the last two years!"

His mind drifted back to the Christmas of '08 almost two full years earlier. He remembered what a nightmare that had been when the devastating aphasia struck him three days before Christmas. He had awakened unable to speak, read, count or write and in a total state of confusion as to what was taking place in his mind and body. The fall from his sleigh which had produced the disabling brain injury had taken his life and his spirits to an all-time low. Not even his darkest days as a prisoner in New York State Penitentiary had taken him to those depths. That he had managed a full recovery was little short of miraculous.

"Thank you, God," he said. He inhaled, then exhaled and with a powerful heave shoved the weight overhead. "Thank you," he repeated. He did several reps before easing the weight back onto the racks and reaching for his towel. He stood up and walked over to his electronic scale as he toweled off his forehead.

The bright red digits seemed to smile at him as he read one-nine-five. Two years earlier, he had weighed in at 345 pounds. In the intervening two years he had dropped 150 pounds and taken his body from total flabbiness to absolute fitness. He was, in every way, a new man—right down to the new, shorter beard. He checked his watch. It was almost time. This was the moment he lived for.

He was beginning to feel the old, familiar adrenalin rush he knew wouldn't end until the last present had been delivered. Only then would he be able to breathe a deep sigh of relief. More than once, the success of the Christmas run had hung by a tenuous thread. By no means was it the given that the general populace seemed to believe and take for granted. He knew from long experience anything could happen and might at any time, wrecking somebody's Christmas. When that happened, the pain was deep and personal. That's why every year's successful run was a personal victory. When he was safely back in the northern fortress, with Marie in his arms and all the staff wildly cheering his triumphant return, he would relax. Meanwhile, until he could proclaim the trip a *fait accompli,* the outcome was problematical. That attitude kept him poised, alert, and prepared for anything.

When it was finished, he and his staff would high five until his hands hurt. They would feast and toast, and he would drink to their health until he ruined his own; but that would come later. Mentally, he slapped himself for his momentary lapse into luxuriating in victory and reminded himself he still had to deal with "now." He picked up the gym's wall phone and dialed Enoch's extension.

Enoch, the head elf and Chief Operating Officer, was his right hand man and the brains behind the *Santa Maria,* the new super sleigh he'd used the past two years. The sleigh was the epitome of futuristic transport and design. From the depths of the earth's oceans, to the upper reaches of the stratosphere and into near space, there was nothing like it. It was a high-tech marvel yet to be fully tested because no one could be found to test it. No one had the strength, reaction speed or physical endurance to take the ship anywhere near its maximum capability and some of its systems had yet to be activated for the first time. Even the elves, who as a species are much stronger and more powerful than men, couldn't take it to the edge and were—wisely—afraid to try.

This time out, the *Santa Maria* was being largely controlled by a new software program.

The phone was finally answered. "Enoch here."

"Are we on track?" Nick asked.

"You know very well that if we weren't on time and on track I would already have advised you."

"How's the new software performing?"

"We've tested everything that could be tested but like all beta versions, it probably has some undiscovered bugs or issues that will have to be addressed."

"Probably has?"

"Make that undoubtedly!"

"I'm glad you're coming along."

"Me too. I don't get out of here often enough."

Nick switched to his employer mode and responded quickly. "There will be no raises or extra vacation time. We just can't afford it right now."

"I was afraid of that."

"And don't tell me that because you're a little guy all you need is a little raise."

"True."

"You do a big job. You deserve a big raise!"

"Also true!"

"But we can't afford it now."

"If not now, then when?"

Nick laughed. "When hell freezes over."

Chuckling, Enoch tried to make himself sound serious, "That soon, huh?"

"That soon; just keep up the good work."

"How you do love to use those four letter words! Did you finish your workout?"

"Indeed I did. When can we leave?"

"I'll check the roster, round up a flight crew and a work crew, and we can be in the air in about six hours. Will that work for you?"

"Fine. Let the team know we have a pre-flight briefing at the hangar thirty minutes before takeoff."

"Check. We'll make that eleven thirty p.m. Greenwich Mean Time at the hangar?"

"Check."

An exhilarated Nick hung up the phone and headed for the shower.

* * * * *

Nick was disturbed. Marie was nowhere to be found. She wasn't in her bedroom, or in the library or the chapel, or anywhere else he had looked. He went to the intercom and hit the master switch. A moment later, his voice crackled throughout the entire compound: "This is the boss. If anyone has seen my wife, please tell her I'm ready to leave and I'd like a kiss and a hug before I go. Got that? Marie, come home! Marie, come home!"

He switched off the intercom. This was totally unlike Marie. Where would she disappear to just before time for him to leave? He couldn't vary his departure routine and leave without a good luck kiss, but five minutes later when she still hadn't appeared, that's exactly what he did.

At eleven fifteen GMT, with his stomach doing flip flops, he got on a snowmobile and headed for the hangar where the crew was gathered for the briefing.

At the hangar, as he stepped off the snowmobile, the diminutive Enoch pounced on him. "Boss..."

"Enoch, I can't find Marie anywhere!"

"That's because she's *here!*"

"She's here?" Nick asked incredulously.

"Just like you're here and I'm here, she's here."

"I should have known," Nick moaned. "When I couldn't find her anywhere else I should have seen this coming. Where is she?"

"She's already on board."

"And the crew?"

"I've already briefed everybody. So just add a few final words and we can be under way."

"I'll talk to the guys after I get her off the ship."

"Good luck."

As they stepped into the huge hangar, all the lights came up, including the running lights on the sides of the *Santa Maria*. As always, Nick paused for a moment to admire the sleek lines of his twenty-second century transport phenom. It wasn't a sleigh; it wasn't an automobile; it wasn't a submarine; it wasn't an airplane or a spacecraft. It was all of those and much more. Enoch and the other designers swore they had borrowed its design and concept from the next century by tying an electromagnetic knot in a two-century time warp they stumbled across while investigating terrestrial magnetic anomalies peculiar to subsurface polar regions. Creating a matching distortion in space, they broke through the interdimensional space-time continuum and pilfered principles of aeronautics design, engineering, and construction not yet delineated in the twenty-first century. It was a classic case of *now* conducting a raid on the *future*. Unusual, but not unknown.

As Nick and Enoch approached the ship, the entire side of the vessel miraculously evanesced and they strode through it as if it didn't exist. Behind them, it rematerialized to become rock-solid once again.

Marie was comfortably ensconced in the same seat she'd occupied two years previously on the ship's maiden voyage when Nick was ill. A half dozen elves occupied the other seats in the command center and were busy with pre-flight checks and planning.

"Oh Nick," she gushed when she looked up and saw him, "I feel *so comfortable* in this seat. I actually think I *missed* it!"

"Don't get too comfortable because you are not coming along on the run."

"Of course I am. That's why I came down a little early for the briefing. I didn't want to miss a thing and I am now fully briefed and ready for the run."

"No. It won't work. You cannot go. You came down early to put me in the embarrassing position of having to publicly deny you or publicly fight with you, but I assure you it will not work. You can't go. Permission denied!"

"Nick!"

"Give me a kiss, get off my sleigh and go home until I get back."

"I can't believe what I'm hearing," she said, about to cry. "My own husband, denying me..."

"Look," Nick said, plopping himself down into the command seat opposite her, "these trips are all dangerous. Anything can happen out there, and I'd never forgive myself if I put you in harm's way. Just go home so I don't have to worry about you."

"So I should go home and stay there and worry about *you?* Listen, I'm down here because I have a bad feeling about this trip. If there's any danger, I'm not letting you go without me."

"Honey, I assure you as Enoch has assured me, everything is in order. We've taken all the usual precautions." He turned to his second in command. "Enoch, please tell her that everything is as it should be."

Enoch sat down in another nearby seat. It automatically lifted to adjust for his weight and height, bringing him closer to the console. Legs dangling, he glanced over the flashing lights and digital readouts, then turned to Marie Claus and reported, "Everything is exactly as it should be, triple-checked, and all appropriate precautions have been taken; redundant back-up systems are in place and functioning properly."

Marie Claus snorted. "Huh! Good try, Enoch. I appreciate your loyalty to Nick, but you're just not a yes-man. You never were and you never will be. Am I right?"

"You're quite right. However, I assure you. We've thought of everything, and done everything we could think of to ensure the safety of the crew and success of the annual mission so..."

Marie was exasperated and beginning to show it. "Spare me the hogwash, Enoch. Your preparations are deficient. Something is wrong! I can *feel* it!"

Santa Claus stood up. "Marie, your imagination is running away with you. I'm about fifteen seconds away from saying, 'No more Mr. Nice Guy,' and giving you something you can *really* feel. Now get off my sleigh!"

"The last time I looked, *your sleigh* had *my* name on it. Anyway, *who* on board is going to put me off? Surely, not you, Mr. Muscles." She stood and assumed her most hostile hands-on-hips posture.

A fuming Nick quickly sat back down. "I knew you were spoiling for a fight. I knew it!"

"Nonsense. I just don't want you to become a statistic. History is replete with stories of great men like yourself who refused to listen to their wives or significant others and suffered dearly for it: Bonaparte, Julius Caesar, and the list goes on and on. Listen to me, Nick. Mine is the voice of love, sent to save you."

"Are you going to get off?" His right leg was bouncing nervously. For a moment, she wondered if he was going to kick her.

"If I get off, I'm afraid that I may never see you again!" She broke into sobs.

A wave of love and compassion swept over Nick as he watched his wife of many years heaving with tears. There was no doubt in his mind he was her sole concern. To her, nothing else mattered as long as he was safe and secure.

"My love won't let me take you and yours won't let me go without you," he said. "I guess that's truly a stalemate, and I really don't know how to break a stalemate."

Marie reached into her purse, pulled out a tissue and blew her nose, then asked, "Are you still a gambling man?"

"I always was and probably always will be. Why?"

"We'll make a little wager. The winner gets his or her way."

"Are we betting on the toss of a coin, or the flip of a card? What are you talking about?"

"Nothing as random as that. This bet has to do with the completeness of your safety equipment and the thoroughness of your preparations. Will you make a bet like that?"

"I will."

Marie leaned close and fixed her eyes on his. "I'm betting that you guys don't even have the protection of a Bible on board this ship."

Santa's gaze never faltered. "Enoch, show her the Bible."

Enoch apparently didn't hear him because he didn't move. Marie continued to stare unblinkingly into Nick's eyes. He spoke again more loudly and with greater authority: "Enoch, please show my wife the Bible then show her the door!"

Enoch cleared his throat before he spoke, "Ahem, boss, there is no Bible."

Marie leaned a few inches closer until her lips softly touched Nick's. "I win," she whispered, "again." Then, pulling back, she called out, "Enoch, I believe we can leave at any time now." She turned to her husband. "Isn't that right, Nick?"

Stroking his shortened beard, Santa Claus acceded, "When were you ever wrong, dear?" He gave Enoch the nod.

* * * * *

Her name was Nightingale, and from the moment he met her, Nick thought the female elf was the most beautiful woman he'd ever seen, bar none. A few months later he met her first cousin, Thrush, whose beauty put Nightingale to shame. Not only were they beautiful, they were both incredibly bright. Any task assigned them was masterfully completed in short order. Santa was well aware they were two of his best employees.

Thrush was actually a chemist by profession. When Nick asked Enoch what use the company had for a chemist, Enoch assured him that her well-rounded engineering skills made her a worthwhile hire and an asset to them. Nick didn't second guess his judgment, and the girl had been a plus from day one.

Nightingale was at the ship's control console and Thrush sat beside her in the copilot/navigator seat, inputting data into the panel which flashed periodically and beeped to acknowledge its acceptance.

Nick turned to his wife and quizzed her: "So, now that you've been briefed, please tell me—if you can—what are our first four continents this evening?"

Marie answered without hesitation, "North America, South America, Antarctica, and then Australia."

"Correct!" he announced. "And now, here is your bonus question. What is our first stop in the U.S.A.?"

"I have no idea."

"That was a bit of a trick question. Please get Freddy on the phone, dear. If he's home, we may pick him up."

He turned to Thrush and Nightingale. "Ladies, set a course for Chattanooga, Tennessee."

Whether day or night, Freddy always answered his phone before the third ring. True to form, he said in crisp voice, "Fred Deere here. How can I help you?" That tone and those words told Nick that Freddy's caller I.D. hadn't identified him.

"How would you like to help me?" he asked jokingly, giving Freddy a chance to recognize his voice.

"Fats!" Freddy exclaimed, "I was just thinking about calling you!"

Nick laughed. "Proving once again that great minds do work together."

"I just wanted to follow up on my note to you, which I'm sure you got. I know you understand that the whole thing was just an unfortunate and innocent mistake, which I *will* take care of. You know *me*."

He was begging forgiveness a little too hard and Nick was reminded of the old saying: "the guilty flee when none pursueth." Nick let his tone turn slightly edgy. "I don't think I got the note that you hadn't yet followed up on. Which of your many unfortunate and innocent mistakes are you speaking of?" He put the call on the speaker.

"Why, the shipment of chips, of course!"

"Of course! Silly me! What's the real story with that shipment?"

"Nick, you know me. I'm just a good ole boy tryin' to make a dollar. One of my prime contacts in Asia gave me his word that those microchips were of impeccable quality at an unbeatable price and could be turned quickly for big bucks. Since I'd never had a problem with any of his merchandise, I bought into the deal. A little later, word began to get back to me that there were some problems..."

"And that's how I got sent some crap that at the very least will cost me time and money, and..."

"Nick, I'm sure that the problems that were reported were not the fault of defective microchips—just buyer's remorse and the usual bellyaching. My guy said they were top quality and I'll stake my life on that!"

"I'm glad to hear you say that, because that's exactly what you're doing. Those chips didn't just go into some toys and games. They went into the mainframe where a system failure could be a threat to life!"

"Huh? I don't understand. What do you…"

"I'm on my way and I'll be there shortly. I'll explain when I see you. Get ready to travel."

"Okay. By the way, I've moved, so let me give you my new address."

"Hey! You still own a firearm don't you?"

"Why, yes."

"Good. Bring it with you."

"You want me to bring a piece? Why?"

"How times have changed! In the old days you were always packing."

"In the old days I needed to stay strapped, but times have changed, Fats."

Enoch whispered in his boss's ear, "The tracking software program places him presently in Coral Gables, Florida, at this address." The street address flashed on a nearby screen, along with several pictures of the house and property.

Nick turned to Thrush. "How long will it take us to get to Coral Gables from where we are now?" He watched her deftly enter the coordinates Enoch had given.

"We're over Chattanooga now," she said. "It's another 712 miles to his location in Coral Gables. We can be there in seven minutes."

"Freddy," Nick said, "be strapped and ready to go in seven minutes. Got that?"

"Seven minutes?"

"You must think time is a magazine or something. You heard me. I'll be there in seven minutes!"

He disconnected the call. "Step on it," he told Nightingale.

They were there in six and a half minutes. Nick hit the redial button on his phone. When Freddy answered, Nick said, "We're in your back yard."

"You must be in the wrong place, Fats. I'm looking right at my back yard and I don't see you."

"We're cloaked, you airhead. Now if you want, we can uncloak, use the holograms to appear as a red and white '57 Chevy, and I'll pull around front and honk the horn for the whole neighborhood to hear! Is that what you prefer?"

"Very funny, Fats. I might be entertained, but I don't know if my neighbors would prefer that."

"If your neighbors knew what I know, they would prefer that you not be a neighbor! Just come out your back door and walk straight down the middle of your back yard until you walk into the ship."

Freddy did exactly what he was told and that's exactly what happened. The side of the craft which he approached should have dematerialized to allow him entry. Instead, it remained invisible and solid as a granite boulder. Freddy walked right into it, bounced backward and fell. Grabbing his nose and sputtering profanity, he tried to regain his feet as Nick stepped from the ship to help him.

"Sorry about that, Freddy. I don't know what happened," Nick said, lifting Freddy as easily as you'd pick up a toddler. He placed him on his feet. "I think our portal malfunctioned."

"Not at all," said Enoch, who by his time had joined them outside the ship. "It did exactly what it was supposed to do. The man is armed. It's inherent in the nature and design of the craft not to admit any weapons or those bearing them. Remember?"

"I'd forgotten. Can we manually override that design feature to get him and the gun aboard?"

"How do you like your 'No?' Long or short? I can give it to you either way."

Freddy was still rubbing his tender proboscis as he tried to speak up. "Surely there must be some way..."

Enoch cut him off at the pass. "There is no way. The transportation of weapons and/or warriors is antithetical to the very peaceful and benevolent purposes for which the craft was designed and created. Inherent in its design is a 'mind'—if you will—of its own. There are certain commands of the operator that it will refuse to obey. Allowing or transporting a weapon is one on them. The ship would implode first. That's your long no."

"Freddy, I'm sorry about your nose," Nick said. "Drop the piece right here and we'll be on our way."

Freddy obediently put the holstered nine millimeter on the ground.

"Follow me," Nick said, stepping through the now-thin-as-air portal and onto the ship.

Freddy tried to follow him only to bump his nose and fall once more. This time he howled in pain and emitted a lengthy string of profanity. In the midst of his pain, what he couldn't believe was the ease with which the elf picked him up and set him back on his feet.

"I think you'll need to leave the spare clip as well," Enoch said.

Freddy pulled bullets and a spare clip from his back pockets and ditched them all in a nearby rose bush. He tried to be careful, but a thorn on the bush drew blood as he secreted his cache of ammo. *Arming and disarming are both hazardous*, he thought.

Enoch stepped aboard, and this time the *Santa Maria* allowed a fully disarmed Freddy to follow.

* * * * *

"Everybody, listen up! Shortly, I'll introduce the gentleman we just picked up. Right now, there are matters of grave importance to be discussed and decided. Nightingale, get us off the ground immediately. Thrush, set a course that will take us directly back to the compound in the event we decide to abandon the North American leg of the run. Marie, please fetch some of Freddy's favorite beverage, and take it and him back to the conversation pit. Enoch and I will be there in a few minutes. Okay, everybody?"

There was a chorus of okays.

Marie and Freddy headed for the conversation pit in the aft of the ship as Nick beckoned to Enoch, who promptly came over.

"Enoch, I hope I'm wrong, but I have the feeling that this computer chip thing could be bad. Am I right?"

"Boss, I hope you're wrong—real wrong. Maybe it's nothing. But you might be real right, in which case it could spell disaster. We need more information."

"That's what I thought. Grab a half dozen or so of our better people and meet me in the back. We'll conduct a thorough interview of Freddy and decide what steps have to be taken." He turned on his heel and headed for the conversation pit.

The conversation pit was their onboard conference room. It was fully reconfigurable at the touch of a button. The plush furniture could be rearranged, the color and lighting scheme changed, and even the wall art and pictures resized or replaced. Stepping into it, you never knew quite what to expect. The walls were also video display monitors for the ship's many short, medium, and long range cameras.

Freddy was in the process of adding more rocks to his scotch when Nick sat down heavily on the couch beside him.

To Freddy's credit, he didn't come close to spilling even a single drop, so dexterously did he manage his glass. Marie poured Nick a big glass of milk and before he could down it, Enoch trooped in followed by six of the crew.

Nick took a big gulp of his milk. "Enoch, you know everybody so why don't you make the introductions?"

"Sure. Everybody, this is Mr. Frederick Rain Deere, an old and dear friend of the boss and his wife." Freddy nodded politely at the cluster of elves seated in a semicircle around him and reached for the bottle to freshen his drink while Enoch continued, "On the far end, we have David and Chester. I believe both you gentlemen will remember meeting Mr. Deere in 2008 on this craft's maiden voyage. That was some trip, wasn't it, guys?"

Both elves smiled and nodded. Enoch continued, "Chester is a senior developer and David is a programmer *par excellence*. They are very intimately involved in all phases of the development of this sleighcraft. Next to Chester is a gentleman we sometimes call 'Confused,' but his real name is Confucius and nothing confuses him. Not only is he a superior technician whose skills span a broad range of applications, he is undeniably one of the best computer hackers in the world. When he was fourteen years old, he went to jail for hacking into the Pentagon's system—repeatedly. He finally left them a note and told them where to find him. They gave him a slap on the wrist and a job. What all he's done since then he doesn't tell and we don't ask. Next to Confucius is Sizzle–"

Nick jumped in, "Sizzle? I thought his name was Fizzle!"

Enoch corrected Nick, "Fizzle is his twin brother who is presently back at the compound. Both are extremely talented psychics, along with their other skills."

"I'm a son-of-a-gun," said Nick. "I didn't know we had any twins at the company."

"We actually have three sets of twins on the payroll."

"Wow! And I thought I knew all my employees."

"Don't worry about it. It would only confuse you. These people can't be told apart by their own parents."

"Psychic twins?" Nick said. "I find that a little hard to believe."

"Oh? Give Sizzle your cell phone." Nick handed the phone over to Sizzle. "Sizzle, contact your brother and tell him to call Nick at that number as soon as he can."

Sizzle looked at the number on the cell phone, then closed his eyes for a few seconds. When he opened them, he said simply, "Done," and handed back the phone. Meanwhile, Enoch continued with the introductions.

"Next to Sizzle is Washburn. He's not a known psychic but he is a well-known genius. So far, his I.Q. has proved immeasurable. He is incredibly gifted. We actually keep him around as a counterweight to some of the institutionalized stupidity present in every organization. As our resident genius, do you have anything to say, Washburn?"

"I say Fizzle isn't going to call. He's going to text, and not be happy!"

Enoch went on. "Saving the best for last, we have the multitalented Thrush."

Her dark eyes were dancing as she smiled charmingly at Freddy, who half stood to extend his hand. "Ah, you're one of the ladies I saw at the command console as I came on board. You do other things as well?"

Enoch finished her introduction. "She is not only a chemical engineer, but she minored in comparative religious studies. She is also a minister. I thought we might need some professional prayer."

At that moment, Nick's cell phone went off. The soft chime instead of the ring told him it was a text message. He flipped it open and read aloud, "I have nothing to prove and I don't like being tested. Fizzle." Nick snapped the phone shut.

Freddy took a sip from his glass and set it down. Fats had always had a knack for surrounding himself with highly talented people, and this current crop might be his crowning achievement. He took another long sip from the scotch and then, looking at Nick over the rim of the glass, said, "I guess I'm not going to be able to call you 'Fats' any more. How much have you lost?"

"Forget my weight loss, Freddy. Let's talk about the problem with the microchips. Tell us what you know about that."

"I don't know much of anything, Nick. I'm *not* a high-tech kind of guy. I only know what I was told. I got a couple of reports..."

Sizzle, the psychic stood up. "A *couple* of reports? Wasn't it more like half a dozen?"

Freddy seemed a little chagrined at being corrected. "Could have been. Anyway, I didn't think they were credible—at least not at first. You guys haven't had any problems, have you, Nick?"

"Not that we yet know of. We need to find out all we can about the microchip fiasco and the problems they caused. Then we need to find out how many *we* used and *where*, and extrapolate from that the possible failure scenarios and potential consequences. We're going to turn Confucius and Washburn loose on your computers, both home and at your office. I assume, of course, that we have your permission?"

"Of course you have my permission. That'll be easier on me. I'm an old man now and my memory isn't what it used to be a few years ago, as you can probably tell. So let your guys have at it. Do they need codes, or passwords?"

Enoch laughed. "Are you kidding? These guys are pros!" He turned to Nick. "Boss, I think we need to put the entire mission on hold until we get some kind of report from our guys."

"You're right. Tell everybody to chill out until we know more."

"I'll pass the word."

Nick turned to the elves. "Thank you, guys. Washburn and Confucius know what to do. If the rest of you can think of anything that needs to be done in the meantime, feel free to do it, but for all practical intents and purposes, the 2010 Christmas run is on an indefinite hold."

The elves quit the room *en masse*. Nick turned to Marie. "We might as well stay right here and get caught up on old times with Freddy." He turned to his old buddy. "Are you hungry? Maybe we can get Marie to fix us a sandwich?" As usual she had anticipated him and was already on the move toward the galley.

"Freddy," Nick said, "come forward with me. I promised the rest of the crew I'd introduce you to them." Freddy followed him forward until he stopped just to the rear of the command center where everyone could see and hear him.

"Listen up, everybody! To those of you who haven't already met him, I want to introduce my oldest and dearest friend, Freddy Rain Deere. I've known him longer than I've known my wife, and I love him more than anybody in the world except my wife. What we've been through together over the years cannot be told." The stentorian level of his volume trailed off a bit as he continued. "Unfortunately, it's in the nature of love—any love—to create problems and pain to balance the joy that it brings. Today, my dearest friend may have brought us some problems—perhaps very serious. We're trying to find out the nature and extent of those and that's the reason for our present holding pattern. Please be patient. We thank you for that and your understanding."

They headed back to the galley where Marie had prepared some sandwiches and fruit. Santa Claus had lost a lost of weight but he still hadn't shed his fat man's appetite and love of food. He was just finishing his second sandwich when Enoch came back and whispered in his ear, "We've got something."

"Great. Let's reconvene our little executive committee back here in ten minutes."

"I'll gather them immediately." Enoch said, already leaving.

Freddy stepped over to Marie and handed her his empty plate. "Thank you, my dear. That was an excellent sandwich." He turned to Nick. "What do we know?"

"We'll have a report in a few minutes," Nick said.

Marie was tidying up the galley. "Honey, what I want to know is what made you think we might need, of all things, a gun? Why did you ask Freddy to bring his firearm?"

"For his own protection, sweetheart," Nick said matter-of-factly.

"My own protection?" Freddy asked quizzically. "From who or what?"

"From me."

"I don't understand," Freddy said.

"Then let me be perfectly clear. If this business of substandard and defective microchips, supplied by you trying to make a few extra bucks, puts my craft and the lives of my crew and wife at risk due to a major system failure caused by hardware meltdown or software failure, or anything related or traceable to those microchips, I plan to break your neck with my bare hands, even as we go down in flames. I wanted you to have the gun so that you might have a fighting chance."

An alarmed Marie cried out, "Nick!"

A bug-eyed Freddy just stared at him and sought confirmation, "Are you serious?"

"Is a massive coronary occlusion?"

"You would kill me?"

"I promise to break your neck with my bare hands!"

"I don't know what to say!"

"There's nothing to be said. Given a meltdown and crash scenario, there are no words of sorrow that could assuage my loss. I would not wish to live even one minute without my Marie; only long enough to avenge her. So you see your greed and recklessness could bring us all face to face with dire consequences."

Marie was crying. "Oh Nick, no."

Nick walked over and gave her a hug, tenderly kissing her eyelids. "I'm sorry, honey."

They were interrupted by the arrival of the elves' executive committee who took up their previous seating arrangement.

"Do I want the good news first or would I rather have the bad?" Nick asked when they were all seated.

Chester answered him, "That's *your* little red wagon. You can push it or you can pull it. Whichever you choose, be assured that the other isn't going anywhere."

"Good, bad—it's all very subjective so who can say what is which or which is what?" David said.

Nick was on the edge of his seat. "Well what did you do? What do we know?"

"Boss, there are no clean, simple answers," Enoch said. "They started with Mr. Deere's computer system and, after ransacking that, they moved on and hacked into the systems of several of his suppliers and their agents and sources, both distributors and manufacturers. Is there a problem? Undoubtedly. Have we somehow fallen heir to it? The best available data suggests that we probably have."

Washburn took over, "Our analysis of the best available data, and hypothetical scientific speculation regarding the unavailable data, lead us unerringly to one conclusion: that nothing can be unerringly concluded. The only thing certain is that there are no certainties. We have built with flawed components, some of which are destined to fail, sooner or later. The M-T-B-F cannot be calculated because..."

"What's M-T-B-F?" Nick asked.

Confucius handled that one, "It stands for mean time before failure, and in some cases, it can be and is possible to calculate. However, there are several complex formulas for calculating it, all of them very suspect. Furthermore, the multitude of factors and variables, both known and unknown, render our present situation absolutely unamenable to any kind of meaningful analysis. We have no idea of exactly what is going to happen or where, or how."

"Can't we model and prepare for some kind or kinds of possible scenarios that we might be able to either avert or handle?" Nick asked, still looking for hope.

"Boss, what they're saying is..." Enoch paused to sip his bottled water, "we've got two chances: slim and none, and Slim is out of town!"

"The scientists aren't holding out much hope, so let me turn to the supernatural," Nick said. "Sizzle, give me your opinion as a professional psychic. What do you see?"

Sizzle closed his eyes and leaned back in his seat. Ever so calmly, he announced, "I see fire and plenty of it."

"You think we're going to crash and burn, or go down in flames?" Nick asked.

"Wrong! Dead wrong!" Enoch said. "This craft cannot burn. Crash, maybe—but burn, no way. Tell him guys."

David and Chester were nodding their heads in agreement with Enoch. "The polymers and materials used in the fabrication of this vessel render it nonburnable under any conditions. That simply is *not* going to happen!" Chester said.

Sizzle defended his vision. "I didn't say I saw the ship in flames or burning. I said, 'I see fire and plenty of it'!"

"Well, as long as it isn't us that's burning," said Nick.

"No, it isn't us," said Sizzle.

"Thrush, speaking as a scientist, do you have anything to add?"

The beautiful young girl, a quiet person by nature, straightened up in her seat. She seemed almost happy to have been invited to participate and voice an opinion. "As a scientist, mathematician and numbers person, no. However, as a theologian and person of faith, I say there is no such thing as a hopeless situation."

"I second that," said Marie, coming to life with the realization that she had at least one ally in faith. "There is always hope!"

"Yes," said Nick, "and a wonderful thing it is. But I like to operate with a greater degree of certainty than that."

"There is nothing more certain than God!" Marie declared. "Absolutely nothing!"

"Let me sum up our situation as I see it, and feel free to correct me if I'm wrong and/or tell me what you think we should do," said Nick. "We're out here a long way from home, on a relatively new sleighcraft, largely untested, equipped with all manner of new and not yet debugged software programs being run by hardware of dubious construction, specifically chips that have known and unknown issues and might fail at any time, bringing about problems ranging from the relatively minor to the catastrophic. If that happens, we can't call Triple A and ask for roadside assistance. There is no one to come to our aid. Dying becomes a distinct possibility. If we carry on and succeed, as always, we will bring joy to many, many people. Some lives will be forever changed. If we don't succeed, the world will go on. It may not be quite as beautiful, but it will continue to exist."

"I've never been a quitter," Chester said, "no matter what the odds. I say we go for it!"

David stood up. "I've never felt that my life was so precious that I was afraid to risk it. Let's go!"

"Fear of death only stops those who are afraid to live," said Confucius. "Now, we can be more alive than ever before."

Nick turned to their resident genius, Washburn. "What do *you* think my friend? Has this venture become too risky for your tastes?"

The immeasurable intellect showed that it was linked to immeasurable heart. "I see no reason why we should be intimidated by the odds against us just because we can't calculate them. I'm in."

"Sizzle?" Nick asked.

"I like delivering gifts and the joy of doing that pleases me. Neither fire nor other unknown hazards is going to stop me."

"Enoch, please give me your take on the situation," Nick said.

"Certainly. We have yet to encounter the first obstacle. Why in the world would we quit now? The only thing we've encountered is the fear of what we might encounter and no one seems intimidated by that. Clearly, we need to move forward and do our job unless or until we no longer can."

"Would you say the consensus is that we should carry on?"

"Absolutely." said Enoch.

"What I don't understand," said Nick, "is who dares to call you all 'little people?' You guys are some of the biggest and bravest men I have ever known. I consider it an absolute honor to be in your company. Thrush, we'll resume the North American leg of the annual run in exactly fifteen minutes, after Enoch completes another systems check. Everybody okay with that?"

There was a chorus of okays.

They uncloaked and put up a hologram presenting the ship as the traditional sleigh drawn by eight reindeer plus a red-nosed Rudolph. The hologram also presented the traditional image of Santa with his pack making each delivery, which actually was performed by an elfin member of the work crew. All the Christmas booty had been infinitized and stored in the cargo hold. At the P.O.D. (Point of Delivery) it was a simple matter for the computer to locate it, bring it forward, deinfinitize it and let a hologram Santa carry it inside. It was very easy, quite quick, and went incredibly well—for the first thirty-seven minutes. Then suddenly the unknown, but not unexpected, arrived.

* * * * *

Nightingale was at the controls. Surprised, she called out, "Enoch! Please come here!"

"Something in your tone tells me that you're the bearer of bad tidings," he said. "What's going on?"

"I was hoping you could tell me," she said, standing up and motioning for him to take her seat. "Have we landed?"

"According to the instruments, we've stopped, but we haven't landed. We're not on the ground, or in the water, nor are we in the air."

"How novel! So where are we and what are we doing?"

"We are nowhere, and doing nothing. Please get Nick."

"I'm already here," said a voice right behind them. "Where are we?"

"Boss, I don't know, and the ship itself doesn't seem to know or if it does it isn't telling."

"You're telling me that *all* our location, GPS and navigation equipment has failed?"

"Yes and no. That may not be the best word. All the readings seem to indicate some kind of overflow."

"I can't see anything out the windows. Is there any indication of danger or hazards if we exit the ship?"

"Not according to the instruments, but then, they may be lying about that as well."

Nick stood up and screamed at the top of his lungs, "SIZZLE! To the command center on the double!"

"You called?" Sizzle said a few seconds later when he appeared from the rear.

"Yes, I did. We need you up here for awhile. Our instruments are giving us false readings or no readings at all. What is your psychic take on that?"

Sizzle closed his eyes for a few seconds, then said, "The instruments are functioning properly."

"What?" Enoch said.

"How can that be?" asked Nick.

Sizzle closed his eyes again and seemed to be gazing deep within. "The instruments and all sensors are functioning as they were designed to function. They cannot communicate to the software the presence of things they were never designed to detect and analyze."

"Wonderful!" said Nick with great sarcasm. "A design flaw. Now, most important of all, are we in any danger if we open or exit the ship?"

This time he was answered immediately. "Not at all."

"Thank you, Sizzle. That will be all for the moment, but don't go too far."

"I won't go anywhere."

Nick turned to Enoch. "Forget the dials and the digital readouts and all that stuff. According to the software, where should we be and what are we doing?"

Enoch typed a few keystrokes on his computer and called up the Master Schedule for North America. "According to the M.S., we're trying to effect a delivery to a thirteen-year-old girl named Janine Jacobs in Springfield, Missouri, and we are either there at her address or the Bird Dog tracking software has followed her to our present location and pinpointed it as the place of delivery."

"Well then, if we're here, let's deliver!" said Nick.

"That's going to be a problem," Sizzle said.

"Why so?"

"Because Janine Jacobs died of cancer three and a half months ago."

There was a long, painful silence as the words sunk in.

"That's not possible," said Enoch. "She couldn't have. If she had died, the scrubbing software would have removed her name from our delivery list."

"That obviously didn't take place," said Nick. "And our present locale is obviously not Springfield, Missouri, which suggests that the amped up delivery and tracking software has followed her to this location, which it doesn't know how to describe or reference in terms of names or mapping coordinates."

"That might explain the overflow readings," said Enoch.

"She's definitely in the vicinity," said Sizzle, "I can *feel* her!"

"Then let's *find* her," said Nick. "Nightingale, open the portal."

When the wall of the ship disappeared, opening to the outside world, not one of them on the sleigh could speak. They were immediately breathless, speechless with wonder at the sight confronting them. They appeared to be in some sort of incredibly lush, primeval, tropical paradise; totally unlike anything they'd ever seen.

Nick thought it was the most beautiful spring day he'd ever experienced. The heady aroma of a thousand different oversized flowers wafted past his nose as a chorus of birds serenaded them on all sides. The sun seemed to be high in the sky, or was it the sun and the moon? He couldn't tell. There was so much light that everything seemed to be shining and shimmering, including the trees and the grass. The sylvan scene of matchless beauty had an instant tranquilizing effect on his soul. Finally, he managed one word.

"Unbelievable!" he said.

Everybody was off the ship and gazing around, lost in their own personal reveries and mentally distant from the task that had brought them there. Suddenly, a man dressed in the whitest white Nick had ever seen appeared at his side and addressed him.

"Are you lost?" the man asked kindly.

"I don't think so," Nick said, "although we're not sure where we are. We were looking for someone."

"You *are* lost, much more so than you realize," said the gentleman in white. "And I fear that you've made a long trip for naught."

"Well if we can find the person we're looking for, it won't all be for naught. I assure you..."

"Nicholas, you are a long way from Springfield, Missouri, and while Janine Jacobs is here, you won't be able to see her."

"Why can't we see her?" Nick asked, resisting the temptation to inquire about the man's obvious knowledge of his identity and more. "Why won't you let us see her?'

"No one here will stop you from seeing her. Only your own eyes, your own mind, your own heart stand in the way of your seeing her."

Nick realized Enoch was standing beside him, and the elf now spoke, "What do you mean?"

As kindly as before, the man in white replied, "Please do not take offense at my words. They are not meant to offend. I practice speaking only the truth and I see that you are from a world that does not take kindly to the truth." He paused for a moment and then nodded his head in the direction of the ship. He asked, "Do you see the city on the other side of your ship?"

"What city?" Enoch asked.

"There's a meadow on the other side of the ship," Nick said, "but no city."

"Be assured," the man said, "that within one hundred yards of your ship there are the first buildings of a magnificent and beautiful city. Those buildings are of alabaster and trimmed in gold and various pastels. I see them clearly. You don't see them at all. To your eyes and mind, they are... I believe you use the word 'cloaked' when you hide your ship. Likewise, the residents of the city are not visible to your eyes. Even if they wish to be seen by you and you wish to see them, the fact of the matter is, you're on different vibratory frequencies. Furthermore, Ms. Jacobs now has everything she ever wanted and more than she or you could ever dream of. She has no need or desire for your presents."

"This is crazy!" said Nick. "We aren't having any trouble seeing or hearing *you*, so why can't we see and talk to *her* if no one is going to stop us?"

"I told you. YOU are stopping you. I have some skills that she hasn't yet developed. I can lower my vibratory rate in order to communicate with you. She's not able to do that, so if you can't raise yours, you can no more see her than you can see those beautiful buildings over there. It's simply a case of mismatched frequencies."

"This is unbelievable," said Enoch. "Where are we? What do you call his place?"

"We have a number of names for it, mostly unknown to you. The one name that you would recognize is 'Heaven'."

Marie began to quietly recite the Lord's Prayer. Thrush had also pulled a rosary from somewhere and seemed to be saying prayers. Nick and Enoch glanced at each other and then back at the white-clad figure.

"You actually expect me to believe that?" said Nick.

"Yes. I am telling you that the pathetically primitive contraption of which you seem so unjustifiably proud has actually brought you to Heaven, and with any luck will start up and take you away so that you can get on with your delivery route. Meanwhile, comfort yourself with the thought that you went to Heaven, even if you couldn't get in. We invite you to return when the purity of your heart, mind, and soul will admit you and render you capable of fully experiencing and enjoying the eternal bliss which the fountain of God's endless and eternal love constantly pours forth in this transcendent realm."

He turned as if to go, then paused and called out, "Marie, please come here."

As she went over to him, he reached into some unseen pocket of his snow white garment and pulled out what appeared to be some type of gold-colored medallion.

"Thank you," she said as he dropped it into her hands. "What is it?"

"Just a little memento from your friends in Heaven, something to keep until we meet again. In an extreme emergency, it could also do double duty and be used as a phone."

"Thank you again, and what is your name sir, if I may ask?"

"You may ask, but my name is not something that's important or that you need to know at this time. Now, get out of here and get your husband back to work, or it could be a long, tough day at the office." He smiled. She smiled. He disappeared into thin air.

"Everybody, back on the ship!" Nick called out and they began to scramble aboard. "Committee meeting in the conversation pit immediately!"

When they were all present and seated Nick asked, "Was I hallucinating alone or did we all hear and see the same things?"

"If it was a hallucination, it was a mass hallucination," said Washburn.

"I think we've just seen and survived our first problem," said Chester, "and it wasn't catastrophic."

"True," said Enoch, "but we still don't know much. We don't know if we're looking at an isolated one time failure of the scrubbing software that just constitutes some kind of anomaly, or if the whole scrubbing program is a failure and nothing can be or has been scrubbed."

"On the other side of the coin, the Point of Delivery and Bird Dog tracking programs seem to be working wonderfully," said Nick. "It tracked a deceased child all the way to Heaven! Who'd have thought it could do that?"

"Over performing can be as bad as under performing," observed Confucius. "I prefer reliability and predictability within the desired parameters of the design."

"Let's see what happens if we continue to push onward. We'll return to our position before the ship stopped. Thrush, tell Nightingale to activate the panel that reads 'Back Track'. That's right, isn't it, Enoch?"

"Yes. That should take us back to our last stop before the incident."

"Alright, and we'll move on from there."

A few minutes later, Nightingale's voice on the intercom announced, "Back Track has returned us to Joplin, Missouri, and is now in a holding mode awaiting further instructions."

"That's where we were before the incident, right?" Nick said, querying Enoch.

"Right."

"Who would ever have thought that Joplin was the last stop before Heaven? Manually delete Janine Jacobs and go to the next name on the list. Cancel Back Track and tell the computer to resume executing the North American distribution. I want another complete system check in forty-five minutes. Can anybody think of anything else we ought to do at his time?"

"Yes," Marie said. "We need to pray."

"I second that," said Thrush.

Nick sat back on the couch and folded his hands. "I am told that the Pilgrims who came to America in the very early days of the country had a motto. It was, 'Pray as if no amount of work would help and work as if no amount of prayer would help.'" He stood up. "Let's get to work, and pray all you like."

* * * * *

The operation ran as flawlessly as a Swiss timepiece for the next twenty-five minutes. Then, out of nowhere, the gremlins were back in the system.

"We're getting that same overflow we had before," Enoch said. "Or if not the same, something analogous or nearly identical to it. The ship doesn't know or can't tell us where we are."

"Is there any environmental data being delivered to us?" Nick asked.

"Not a shred or a smidgeon."

"According to the Master Schedule on North America, exactly where should we be?"

"Thrush, would you please call Sizzle again, and check the M.S. on North America," Enoch said. "This could quickly get old."

"According to the Master, we're trying to deliver to Aloysius P. Johnson in Santa Rosa, New Mexico."

Sizzle appeared and seated himself. "Same scenario, huh?" he asked.

"Virtually identical," Enoch told him. "We're looking for an Aloysius P. Johnson in Santa Rosa, New Mexico. What's your feeling?"

"My feeling is that we're going to find Aloysius very soon."

"Are we anywhere near Santa Rosa, New Mexico?" Nick asked.

"No way!" Sizzle responded.

"We can't see or detect anything about the outside. If we open the ship or go out, is there any danger?"

"There is no immediate danger, though there *is* danger," was Sizzle's response.

"Danger, but not immediate..." Nick repeated. "That means we can escape it, or that we have time to respond to the threat and handle the situation."

"I would concur with that assessment," said Enoch. He turned to Sizzle. "And you think we're going to locate Aloysius P. Johnson, huh?"

"There's no question that he's here. Our Bird Dog tracking software is working well. Of course, maybe his name should have been scrubbed and wasn't."

"Do you think he's alive and well?" Nick asked.

"He's neither."

"What do you mean?"

"I mean he died two months ago."

"Are you trying to tell me that we've tracked another dead person—to some unknown realm?"

"Yes and no. That he died, affirmative. That we've tracked him to an unknown realm, unconfirmed. My spirit guides say open the ship and you'll know where we are."

Nick gave the order, "Nightingale, open the portal!"

The molecular dispersion of the sleigh's wall as it once again evanesced treated them to a singularly stunning sight. It was more stunning than the previous first view of Heaven. If there's anything more stunning than the first view of Heaven, it's the first glimpse of Hell. Clearly. shockingly, and undeniably, they were in Hell!

Sizzle's previous prediction about "fire and plenty of it" came immediately to mind as they gazed at a mountain of flame some distance away. To a person, they were in shock. No one had anything to say. There was nothing to be said.

Nick personally hoped since they hadn't seen God in Heaven, maybe they wouldn't see the Devil in Hell. But there was no question in his mind that Hell was where they were. There was the pungent odor of sulfur in the overheated, smoky air, and the distant glow of what could only be flames spanned every horizon. In the distance, Nick thought he heard screams and tortured cries. His heart began to pound and the hair rose on the nape of his neck as the full realization sunk in.

"Sizzle," Enoch said, "are you sure that Mr. Johnson is here?"

"Yes, and we'll see him very soon."

"How will we find him?" Thrush asked.

"We'll be taken to him."

"By whom?" Nick asked. "Who will guide us to him?"

Close by, a booming voice responded to his question, "Why *me* of course! I will!"

They all turned to see a rather tall man, immaculately clad in a well-tailored bright red, three-piece suit with matching red shirt and tie standing just outside the ship.

"Welcome, and do come out," he said. "You don't need to take your shoes off. This is not hallowed ground."

There was something about the man that seemed strangely familiar to Nick, but he couldn't place him, so he asked, "Who in the hell are you?"

"I am the Chief Guide in Hell. That's who I am. I can take you to anyone who's here or tell you all about anyone who's ever been here and those who are coming or expected."

"Impressive," Nick said as he stepped off the ship and the others began to follow. "And your name is?"

"Come now, Nick. Surely, you remember me. I certainly remember you, and by the way, let me congratulate you on the choice of color for your suit. That scarlet is beautiful. But I must tell you, that style went out with high button shoes. We're going to have to find you a new tailor."

"Thank you for the kind offer, but I have no interest in sartorial elegance. I'm only here to find a Mr. Johnson. Aloysius Johnson."

"Middle initial 'P'?"

"Why, yes!"

"Of course. Aloysius P. Johnson, Senior Deacon of the First United Pentecostal Church of Santa Rosa, New Mexico, has been with us for a couple of months now. What a man! In twenty-five years, they never once passed a collection plate that he didn't have his fingers in, and as a master pitch man— excuse me, orator—and one of the founding fathers of that congregation, he could..."

"Spare us the accolades. Where is he?" Nick demanded.

"Why right now, he's trying to enjoy a nice cool drink of ice water. Do you want me to take you to him?"

"Please."

"Just follow me. It isn't far. We can take the whole crew. Bring anybody who wants to see what we're all about here. Many people don't believe that there is ice water in Hell, but I can assure you that there is."

Everyone wanted to go on the little jaunt and see the ice water in Hell. "Maybe we should leave a skeleton crew here to guard the ship," Enoch suggested.

"With what weapons?" Nick asked. "I feel better about everyone's safety if we're all in one group." They closed and locked the ship and all traipsed off following the Chief Guide.

A quarter mile hike over volcanic rock brought them to a plateau which proved to be an overhanging escarpment from which they could look down on a vast and incredible scene of punishment and torture. As far as the eye could see, there were people, humanoids and even some animals, evidently in unbearable pain. The air was rent with their shrieks and anguished cries at the unremitting torture they suffered. A foul, odoriferous stench, as of sulfur and burning flesh, hung heavily in the rank atmosphere. The oppressive heat was heavier than a medicine ball.

"Deacon Johnson is over there," said the Chief Guide, pointing to one lone man trying repeatedly to climb a small hillock.

The hill itself didn't appear to be that challenging because of the grade, but it evidently had some very hot spots which Johnson had to dodge and work around as he made his way up.

At the very top was a spigot and water. Apparently cold water poured from it into, of all things, a metal church collection plate. In order to reach the plate, Johnson had to stretch out his arms and reach across what appeared to be about a three to four foot wide ditch. Whenever he tried to pick up the water-filled plate, its contents would spill onto hot rocks in the ditch below and a huge blast of steam would rise up and hit him in the face, invariably tumbling him back down the hill—burned, bruised, and still thirsty. He would start all over only to repeat the entire futile exercise. He couldn't stop.

The Chief Guide laughed. "That's some great water if only he could get to it. Some of the best ice water in Hell, but no one seems to be quite able to reach it, or hold on to the hot collection plate and get a cool, refreshing drink."

"Can he come up and talk to us?" asked Marie.

"Absolutely not!" said the Chief Guide. "The comfort of visitation is not allowed. Nor are breaks. Any such conduct would be in violation of the rules!"

"Rules?"

"Hell is not a lawless place," said the Chief Guide. "This is not the old, wild west. There are rules and regulations. Now, while he can't come up here, you *can* go down there. However, I don't recommend it."

"Why not?" asked Enoch.

"You become subject to a different set of laws. The rules change."

"To hell with that," said Nick.

"Thank you," said the Chief Guide, smiling.

"Boss... Boss!" Enoch's voice had a frantic edge. "I just got a message from the *Santa Maria!*"

"What? How can that be? We weren't getting anything but overflow readings before, or when we arrived here."

"I think some of the software may have auto-reset and is now reading and transmitting. Anyway, the ship is reporting a very high external temperature. We need to get back there immediately to see what's going on!"

"Everybody, back to the sleigh!" Nick screamed, "Right away!" They all took off running in the direction of the sleigh.

Well before they got there, they could see the flames. When they arrived on the spot, flames were so high they actually couldn't see the ship. Nick ran completely around the perimeter of the blaze.

"Looks real bad, Enoch," he said. "I'm not sure what we can do, if anything."

"Let's move the ship!" Enoch said.

"Try it. Move it 100 meters to the south."

A few seconds later, Enoch activated the remote command. The sleigh rose straight up several feet into the air, shuddered briefly like a living thing convulsing in its death throes, then dropped heavily back down into the raging fire, where it sat, immobile.

The crew watched the unapproachable blaze, helpless, as Nick got nose to nose with the Chief Guide. "Who set fire to our ship?" he demanded.

"How would I know?" said the Chief Guide. "I was with *you*!"

"You know everything that goes on here! Now I wanna know who set fire to our ship?"

"Let me disabuse you of certain notions," said the Chief Guide. "First of all, I don't know *everything* that takes place. Hell is a huge realm, and this is just the first of seven levels, each of which gets progressively worse than the previous level. The imps or any wandering miscreant demons might have tried to burn up your ship. That's not an impossible scenario. But what is more likely is that the natural laws of Hell, which operate differently from the natural laws of earth, acted to attempt the destruction of your ship."

"What? What do you mean?"

"Spontaneous combustion. I already told you that Hell has its own laws. Frequently, here in Hell, things just erupt into flames, for no apparent reason other than that is the natural law of this realm. Moreover, your ship is *not* on fire or burning."

"Huh?" said Nick.

"He's right, Boss," said Enoch. "Didn't you notice when the ship rose up out of the flames, it wasn't on fire? Even now, it's sitting in fire and is surrounded by flames, but the craft itself is *not* burning. The *Santa Maria* is not on fire."

Nick was speechless, but the Chief Guide and Enoch were correct. The flames burned down and then went out. When the smoke cleared, the *Santa Maria* was unscathed.

"The Executive Committee is now in session," Nick declared when they were all back on board the ship. "Ladies and gentlemen, can I get a group opinion on how fast we should try to leave here?"

"Immediately if not sooner," said Confucius.

"That's too long," said Chester.

"Faster than ASAP!" said Thrush, and Nightingale nodded her agreement.

"Good. I think we're all agreed," said Nick. "Enoch, give us some kind of system check and then we're out of here."

David stood up. "There is one item that we should probably take care of before we go."

Enoch was leaving to begin the system check. He paused, "Which is?"

"We need to disable the Bird Dog tracking program which seems to be working too well, and maybe all the new software that we're uncertain about. Since the scrubbing software has not purged certain names from the list, we don't know how many more times we might wind up back here, or worse yet, deeper in Hell if such a thing is possible."

"Oh it's possible," said Enoch. "The Chief Guide was very clear about that."

"Disabling all that software may really jeopardize the remainder of the run," said Nick. "I really hate to do that."

"The remainder of the run is in jeopardy anyway," said Enoch, "if we have any more problems at all."

"I don't care if the run is in jeopardy as long as *you* aren't," Marie said to Nick and gave him a kiss on the cheek.

"So be it. Enoch, you, David and Confucius take care of disabling the nonessential software. I'll do a quick check of the exterior with Chester and then we'll say goodbye to Hell."

The Chief Guide was waiting on him when he and Chester exited the ship for their inspection. Seated casually atop a big

C.E. MALLORY

boulder, he was picking his teeth with a red plastic toothpick. "Why do I feel like you're anxious to leave us?"

"You're terribly intuitive," Nick said, "and I thank you for your assistance. Nevertheless, we do have a schedule to keep and so, regrettably, we must be on our way."

"But you'll miss the reunion party that we were planning for you!"

"What reunion party?"

"Why, the one with some of your old friends. They do so want to see you, and Mr. Deere, of course!

"What old friends?"

"Wentworth, Robish, and their associates. Not to mention Do-Wah-Ditty and Wobblehead."

"Those names mean nothing to me." Nick said.

"I do swear, your memory may not be fully recovered from the aphasia incident if you don't remember these people. But Mr. Deere will remember them, I'm sure."

"Freddy, come out here please," Nick called. Freddy appeared momentarily, with a water glass in his hand, but it wasn't filled with water.

"Freddy, Mr. Chief Guide here says that if we leave, we'll miss a reunion party that some of our old acquaintances are looking forward to staging for us. I don't remember the people he's talking about and doubt that I ever knew them. He says your memory is better than mine and you'll recall them. Give him the names, Mr. Chief Guide."

"Surely you remember these two gentlemen, Mr. Deere. One was named Wentworth and his partner was a Mr. Robish."

"Wentworth and Robish. Wentworth and Robish…" Freddy repeated the names trying to force his memory to kick in. "WENTWORTH AND ROBISH!! Are they here?" Freddy asked incredulously.

"For sure."

"Robish! I hated that red-headed bastard with a passion. Even worse than I hated Wentworth. Nick, surely you recall those—just think of the two most worthless pieces-of-crap individuals you have ever known and they will come immediately to mind. God, Nick! Why didn't you let me bring the piece? If I had my nine millimeter we could settle some old scores."

"Wait. Aren't those the two New York City detectives who hassled us so in the early sixties?"

"You bet your sweet bippy!"

"We were paying those guys off along with half their precinct and they double-crossed us and busted us anyway!"

"That's them!"

Nick put his hand over his heart. "Freddy, as a Christian, I like to think that I have long since forgotten and forgiven those scurrilous bastards." He turned to the Chief Guide. "Who were the other two names you mentioned?"

"Do-Wah-Ditty and Wobblehead."

Freddy came close to choking on his scotch. "Do-Wah-Ditty and Wobblehead! Nick, you've really lost it if you don't remember Do-Wah-Ditty and Wobblehead. Think Attica! Think Sing Sing!"

Nick almost said, "Oh my God!" but he had trained himself not to take the Lord's name in vain so he settled for something less offensive to the universe.

"The last time you probably saw them," said Freddy, "was the day you broke out of Sing Sing. Those punks were the ringleaders of a plan to hold a little shiv party for you. And you were going to be the only one there without a shiv. I didn't hear about it until after you were gone. Of course, by then, it would have been too late. You'd have been yesterday's chopped liver!"

Nick winced at the memory and threw up his hands in painful despair. "See, Freddy," he accused, "if you'd just brought your piece like I told you, we could really have some fun at that reunion party!"

"But you're a Christian," Freddy said.

"So what? Shooting bastards who've already gone to Hell doesn't count against you. I would think of it as a sort of symbolic re-killing—confirmation of their original worthless, jackass scum status. Fortunately, or unfortunately as the case may be, we're not armed, nor do we have time to settle old scores." Nick turned. "Unfortunately, Mr. Chief Guide, we'll have to pass on the reunion party. I'm sure you understand."

"No, frankly I don't. Why even leave? In your heart of hearts, you know you'll be back. Sooner or later, the two of you are fated to return! It's your destiny!" He turned to Nick. "Memory is bi-directional. When we first met, you recognized me. You remember me from the future."

"Is that a wish or a prediction?" asked Freddy, finishing off the remainder of the scotch.

"Neither. It's just a simple statement of fact. *If* you leave here, you *will* be back."

"What do you mean by *if*?" said Nick. "I already told you, we're leaving."

"Many a slip betwixt the cup and the lip, my friend. You're not gone yet."

"We'll happily accept that as a fond farewell. So until we meet again..."

"We won't. When you next come back to Hell, you won't be seeing *me*!"

"No? Too bad. Well, in the words of Willie Shakespeare, 'Parting is such sweet sorrow,' and now we must be off."

Nick and Freddy stepped back into the ship as the portal closed soundlessly behind them.

"Good riddance!" said Freddy

"Enoch, are we ready?" Nick called out.

"All systems are ready, Boss!"

"Then let's get the hell out of here!"

"Check."

* * * * *

Fifteen minutes later, when the *Santa Maria* still hadn't been able to take off, Nick reconvened the Committee.

Enoch looked at Nick and shrugged his shoulders hopelessly. "Boss, I don't know what to say. We've done the complete system check three times. Everything is in perfect order. We even tried enabling the suspect software that we disabled. It doesn't seem to matter. This craft is not going to fly and I don't know why."

"It's crazy," Washburn said.

Nick turned to Sizzle. "Science, engineering and technology are disappointing me, Sizzle. Please give me your psychic perceptions of what is happening or is going to happen."

"It apparently has to do with the laws of Hell. There is nothing wrong with the ship."

"I don't know if that's good or bad," said Nick.

"Neither do I," said Sizzle. "But apparently, in Hell, we are subject to all the laws of Hell."

"How much danger are we in?"

"There is danger and it is growing. I see fire and plenty of it. Furthermore..." he hesitated.

"Furthermore what?"

"We're going to lose someone."

"You mean lose as in die?"

"Yes."

"No!" said Marie.

Nightingale gasped and then began to weep.

"We cannot let that happen," said Nick. "It must be prevented at all costs."

"It may be unpreventable," said Sizzle.

"Life is uncertain," said Confucius stoically. "Death is sure."

"After the first death, if we don't get help, or figure out a way to leave here, then one by one we will all die," said Sizzle. "It won't be pretty."

Nick turned to Enoch and sighed. "I'd give anything to be able to call Triple A and ask for roadside assistance."

"Likewise," said Enoch.

"Do you think there's anybody back at home who might know or be able to suggest something we can try?"

"I don't know," said Enoch. "We've got our very best people with us. Still, you never know. I don't know if we can even make any contact from where we are. And since we're not yet overdue, they probably aren't trying to contact us. And unless and until we fail to return, they won't be looking for us.

And should they, what are the chances of them locating us in Hell?"

Nick allowed himself a moment of cynicism. "Thank you. I needed to see the situation in its most positive light." He contemplated a moment. "Sizzle, please try to reach your brother and explain our situation. If you can, maybe he or someone else there in the compound can make a suggestion or come up with an idea. There must be *something* they can do."

"Right," Sizzle said, nodding and shifting his position in the chair. "Give me a moment." He closed his eyes and became very still.

Three minutes later he exclaimed, "This is amazing!" When he opened his eyes, it was evident he was perplexed. "I don't ever remember *not* being able to reach my brother. It's as if there's some kind of insuperable wall that I can't penetrate."

"You can't reach Fizzle?" Enoch asked.

"Not at all. It's almost as if he was dead, or maybe I'm dead?"

"You're not dead," Nick said, "Not yet. Hey, somebody open the portal."

The Chief Guide was waiting on Nick when he stepped off the sleigh. "You changed your mind about the reunion party?" He smiled. "I was hoping you would."

Nick chose to ignore that and go right to the point. "You knew we wouldn't be able to leave, didn't you?"

"I didn't know for certain, but I suspected as much."

"You might have told us." Nick accused.

"It wouldn't have helped or mattered. Even now, if I explained to you all the laws of Hell, it wouldn't matter. Hell is not something you can be taught. You experience it and learn it on your on. You're already learning. Right now, you've learned that getting into Hell is very easy. Getting out is another matter altogether. Those are the rules of Hell. Anybody can get in. Nobody can leave."

"Are you trying to tell me that we're not going to be able to leave?"

"I'm telling you that you're free to leave at any time, if you can manage it. However, that's easier said than done. You probably can't even get a message through to anyone who would be able to help you, if there was such a thing as 'hope' of help for those in Hell."

"Are we captives?"

"Not at all. Just because you can't leave doesn't make you a captive. It's just that coming into Hell is a little bit like walking into quicksand. One, maybe two steps, and you're hopelessly mired. The harder you struggle to get out, the faster you sink."

"What, specifically, is actually keeping us here?" Nick demanded.

"I would say that a combination of forces, both natural and supernatural, are acting upon you and have you bound. The present situation is possibly only temporary, but it may well become permanent."

Enoch had been listening to the entire conversation from his position just inside the portal. "Why would it become permanent?" he asked.

"Because change is a law of life, even in Hell. Nothing stays the same. Things are always changing. Here in Hell, that usually means that your situation is getting worse."

"Why so?" asked Nick.

"Again, I invite you to look to nature. In nature, struggle always invites attention. Often, that is the unwanted attention of predators. You're struggling. Physically, mentally and emotionally. As with any trapped animal, not only will those struggles weaken and exhaust you, they will draw unwelcome predatory attention. The best example of this is an insect that has landed upon a spider's web and become stuck and then entangled. His frantic efforts to break free vibrate the entire web and alert the spider to the presence of a victim. The dinner bell has rung."

"An interesting if rather grim view," said Enoch.

The Chief Guide continued, "Bear in mind many thousands of people come to Hell every day. Without exception, they all want to leave. The problem for all of them is that they can't leave because they have earned their residency. You people, on the other hand, have not done that—at least not yet, though some of you are working on it. Therefore, since you've earned no spot, Hell has no claim on you, leaving you free to depart, if you can manage to do so. Sooner would be better than later."

"Oh?" said Enoch.

"As you can imagine, we don't get many true visitors. Already, you've come to the attention of my higher-ups. They might decide to summon you at any time. That meeting does not bode well for you."

"Would they send you or someone else to bring us to them?" asked Nick.

"The powers that rule Hell do not require the services of third parties to execute any summons. When they want you, you WILL be brought before them. You have no choice, you have no options, you have no power to resist. It's very simple, cut and dried. Also, unlike any earthly judicial proceedings, you have no rights."

"And suppose we *want* to see your higher-ups; can that be arranged?" asked Nick.

"I would caution you to be careful what you ask for."

"Sounds like good advice to me," said Enoch. "Thank you!" He promptly retreated back into the safety of the ship.

"I didn't mean to frighten the little fellow." The Chief Guide smiled to Nick after Enoch left.

"Oh, you meant to, but you didn't and you can't," said Nick. "You see, inside that small, slight body beats a mammoth heart. Neither you, nor all the demons you could muster can intimidate that elf."

"Then he, like Santa Claus, is just another doomed, moribund hero," said the Chief Guide. "Both of you are rushing headlong into the outstretched arms of death!"

Nick returned to the conversation pit where Enoch, Washburn, Chester, David and Confucius were analyzing the problem based on the information the Chief Guide had imparted.

Nick told Enoch, "He thinks he scared you."

"Oh yeah? Tell him to try me again at Halloween. He might have better luck."

"We're the ones who'll need the luck. Especially if we can do what I think we should," said Nick.

"Which is?" said Chester.

"Request a meeting with Mr. Chief Guide's big boss."

"Boss," said Enoch, "no disrespect intended, but have you lost your mind? We don't know exactly who the 'higher-ups' are or might be. You could be asking for a face-to-face meeting with the Devil himself!"

"I hope not," said Nick. "Granted, it might be a case of 'out of the frying pan and into the fire,' but..."

"What would we hope to gain from such a meeting?" asked Washburn.

"I don't think we're going to be able to leave on our own or break out of here. Our best chance is to have them decide to put us out."

"First we go to Heaven and we can't get in," said Confucius. "Now you want to get us expelled from Hell."

"I think it's our only chance."

"There's no such thing as an *only* chance," said Confucius. "Circumstances are the parents of chance, and if they give birth to one, then like all parents, they can give birth to a couple more."

"It's too risky," said David. "There's just too much we don't know about Hell. We might not ever get face-to-face with a higher-up. We might not even be able to survive a harsher environment. Our bodies can stand only so much smoke and toxic air, and we have no idea what the ship can bear."

"All good questions and deserving of answers, which I have a feeling we'll discover soon enough," said Nick.

"We know what Sizzle's feelings are based on: his tremendous psychic intuitiveness. What is the basis of your feeling?" asked Chester.

"I feel it in my bones. My arthritic old bones, sensitive to air pressure and pressure changes and such, are signaling me that something is happening. I feel it in my bones. Are we able to get any kind of readings?" Nick asked.

"None that I would trust," said Enoch. "For instance, right now our altimeter—which wasn't working at all—is now

C.E. MALLORY

reading an unbelievable negative 132,000 feet below sea level. That would put us over twenty-five miles under ground, and the reading is still falling. You see why I don't trust it?"

"You built this ship and *you* don't trust the instruments?" Nick asked.

"Given the present circumstances, no," said Enoch.

"Can't you feel the pressure changing? My joints, my bones, are actually hurting," said Nick as the altimeter continued to climb. Finally, it began to slow and stopped at minus one hundred ninety-eight thousand feet.

"If that gauge is to be believed, we're thirty-seven and one half miles below the surface," said David.

"I don't believe it," said Chester.

"I do," said Nick.

"Hell," said Enoch, "is full of lies and liars, and I think the altimeter just joined the Liars Club!"

"That device is right on," said Washburn.

"No way!" denied Confucius. "It's not possible. None of this is possible! There cannot be any subsurface life or life forms. It's broken."

"So then, what exactly is it reading?" asked Nick.

"How the devil should I know? For all I know, it's reading the alcohol content of your friend's blood! That should be getting pretty high by now, too!" Confucius had raised his volume considerably and was obviously agitated.

"We all need to remain calm," Nick said. He turned to his old friend. "Freddy, I know you're not a member of the crew, but your life is on the line along with the rest of ours so we welcome any input you might have to offer, and that input might be more meaningful, valuable, and better received if you lay off the sauce."

"I am, and will remain, as sober as a judge," said Freddy.

"I wasn't suggesting that you were drunk," said Nick.

"Drunken mind speaks with sober thought," said Freddy. "If we actually are on the Devil's doorstep, it may be that the spirit of evil has already begun to attack our ship and everybody on it. It *may* be that under the Devil's influence and control, all the sensory and monitoring devices are misreporting or lying. The Christian folk have long said that the Devil is the father of lies. Where I come from, we just say, 'The Devil is a friggin' liar!'"

"Can we see anything out the portal?" asked Enoch. "Anything in any direction?"

"North, south, east and west we have zero visibility," said Thrush.

"Sizzle, is there any life out there?" asked Nick.

"There is life out there; there is death out there; and then there are the living dead, those not clearly in either group."

"What more do you see?"

"Again, I see fire and plenty of it."

"How much danger are we in?" Nick asked quietly.

The answer came loudly and without hesitation: "Plenty!"

"If we open the portal and exit the ship, are we all struck dead or something?"

"No. The threat is not that immediate."

"Can we find someone in authority to talk to?"

"They'll find *you*!"

Nick sighed heavily. "What has to happen before we can leave here?"

Now it was Sizzle's turn to sigh. "Someone must die!" he said.

* * * * *

When they opened the portal, the hideous beauty of the firescape which confronted them to the east was unlike anything they'd ever seen. Tongues of flames as high as a skyscraper licked hungrily at the stygian blackness of a starless sky as mountainous waves of pure fire coursed to and fro. The blast furnace heat pummeled them with the relentless fury of a mixed martial arts fighter, as they gasped for every breath, each of which seemed certain to be the last.

On the western side of the ship, a pathetic herd of sullen-faced humanoids stared at them out of lifeless eyes, milling about incessantly without purpose or plan.

Sheeple! thought Nick.

Here and there in the milling herd, occasionally someone would fall down, only to be trampled by the rest, until his agonized cries ceased. On the perimeter of the herd, half man half wolf creatures seemed to have the role of shepherds, moving the herd of sheeple at their will and occasionally running in to seize one.

As the crew watched in horror, the wolf-men shepherds seized a victim. There was an obvious sense of glee as they subjected the hapless victim to a brutal group sexual assault, then clawed him apart with their bare hands and began a voracious feed on the protruding viscera. It wasn't a pretty sight. Several crew members lost the contents of their stomachs.

"Enjoying the show?" said a voice close at hand. Nick looked around to see who might have addressed him, but could see no one. Freddy was the closest person to him. He thought it might have been Freddy who spoke, so he answered.

"No Freddy, I'm not enjoying the show. How any human being could ever enjoy such brutality is beyond me."

It was the response that made him realize Freddy wasn't the speaker. "We have many forms of entertainment and diversion here in Hell. After all, many of those who come here have spent their lives seeking entertainment and diversion. Is it not fitting that they should ultimately spend their deaths similarly engaged, even in a participatory role?"

"Who *are* you?" said Nick. "And *where* are you?"

"Why, I'm one of the 'higher-ups' you said you wanted to see, and I'm right here with you. Is that a surprise?" said the disembodied voice.

"Not exactly what I was expecting," said Nick. "Do you have a name?"

"My name is none of your business. However, you can call me D.A."

"Well D.A., I'm pleased to meet you, if this can be said to be a meeting."

"Don't be too pleased too soon. Most people who meet me usually have cause to regret it sooner or later. Incidentally, for your information and edification, D.A. does not stand for

District Attorney as in the world you come from. Rather, it means that I am the Devil's Advocate. You may have been a skilled escape artist in your time, but we are singularly unimpressed by your legendary antics on the planet's surface. The rules here are different, and I can assure you, you will not escape the clutches of Hell!"

"Nick, are you talking to someone?" asked Freddy, moving a couple of steps closer.

"Yes," said Nick. "I'm talking to the invisible Mr. D.A. He's one of the Chief Guide's higher-ups."

"Well Mr. D.A., are you going to release us?" Freddy asked hopefully of the disembodied voice.

"Why should we? We did not intricate you in Hell's affairs. Therefore we are under no obligation to extricate you. You can all rot in hell as far as I'm concerned. We may use some of your little people as new breeding stock for the imps. Those elves seem to be a hardy bunch. If we can breed out some of the genetic flaws relating to inherent goodness, they might make worthwhile miniature demons. As for the rest of you, I'll spit on your putrescent corpses before I consign you to the flames."

"You diabolical bastard!" said Freddy.

"What did you expect? Mercy?" said D.A. "'The Devil is a friggin' liar,' remember? This is Hell. There is no charity here. There is no mercy!"

"Then screw you and the horse you rode in on!" shrieked Freddy.

"We'll see who's screwed!" said D.A.

Freddy's outburst drew everyone's attention, and Nick walked over to talk to Marie. "Honey, it doesn't look like it's going to go well. I spoke..."

"What's wrong with him?" she asked, nodding at Freddy.

Freddy was turning around in circles. He seemed disoriented. "Fats," he said, "I feel strange."

"Are you sick?" Nick asked

"No... Yes... Maybe not. I don't know." A strange blue light seemed to flash around his body. "I feel very funny."

"You look a little out of sorts," said Nick. "Why don't you go lie down for a bit?"

"Good idea," said Freddy. He took two steps toward the ship before his legs buckled. He went down on his right knee, with his left leg bent at the knee and his left foot still flat on the ground. Without a trace of warning, his body suddenly erupted into a horrific mass of flames.

"Quick!" shouted Nick, "Bring a fire extinguisher!"

"There aren't any!" screamed Enoch. "Can we wrap him and roll him?"

They couldn't. There was far too much flame, burning far too intensely, and with such ferocity that it was all completely over in less than two and a half minutes. Frederick Rain Deere, aka "No Questions Asked Freddy," also known as "Freddy the Fence" was totally incinerated and reduced to mere ashes in the space of 150 seconds. In full view of twenty-four panicked people who watched helplessly, he burned so totally that there were not even skeletal remains, other than his lower left leg and his right knee. Amazingly, his body had remained in that position of kneeling on one knee all the while the flames were consuming it. Not until they tried to move it did the corpse crumble into ashes.

The entire crew was in total shock. Most of them had never even heard of S.H.C. much less witnessed it. Now, suddenly brought face to face with it, they were all believers in Spontaneous Human Combustion. Each of them wondered, *Could that happen to me?*

For no apparent reason, one of their own had, without any source of ignition or accelerant, exploded into flames and burned so intensely that within a couple of minutes his entire body was reduced to a knee, one lower leg, and a pile of ashes. It was shocking. It was frightening, and it was true. Death was no longer an abstraction. Today, death was real.

Nick was in major shock along with everyone else. No one seemed to know what to do. Nick had no idea what to say. None of their plans had ever included any "death contingency." All three of the women were crying unabashed tears, as were a number of the male elves. A palpable, icy fear gripped the hearts of one and all.

Twenty minutes later, they were back on board the ship and in the conversation pit. A very shaken Marie said, "Thrush, could you please hand me my purse? I need to get my Bible."

"Sure." Thrush promptly handed Marie the purse. For a rather small handbag, the purse contained a rather large Bible. Marie moved to open the Bible and that's when the gold medallion fell out from between the pages. After the man in white gave it to her, she had tossed it into her purse and promptly forgotten about it. Now, seeing it lying there gleaming on the table she remembered his words: "In an extreme emergency, it could also do double duty and be used as a phone."

Used as a phone? she thought. *How do I do that?* She had no idea. Besides, she just wanted very much to pray. She was clutching the medallion tightly in her fist as she started to recite the Lord's Prayer.

"Our Father, who..."

"Marie!"

Completely startled, she jumped. "Oh my!" she said to the bearded, middle-aged man suddenly sitting on the couch beside her. "You scared me! Where did *you* come from?"

"Just now? About halfway across the Milky Way Galaxy." He smiled.

"That can't be. Halfway across the Milky Way Galaxy is many, many, light years away."

There was a bit of a twinkle in his deep-set, gray eyes, "Very good, Marie! Your knowledge of astronomy is not astounding, but certainly there's hope for you." Now he laughed, and that relaxed her a bit.

"My knowledge of astronomy is rudimentary and likely to remain that way," she said, "but I do know such an incredible number of light years is not a distance anyone could ever traverse. Even at the speed of light..."

"Please allow me to help you expand your rudimentary knowledge. There are no *incredible* or unbelievable numbers, it *is* a traversable distance, and I *do not* travel at the speed of light.

"Who *are* you?" she finally asked, thoroughly befuddled by his statements.

"You can call me Mr. E. I'm here in response to your call."

"But how can that be? I only said two words."

"Your mistake is your belief in sequential moments. You think that your moment of need, your moment of prayer and supplication to God, the moment of Heaven's response, and the time of my arrival are each separate moments. That is incorrect. In God's eternal now, they are all the same moment. One and the same."

"Mr. E.," she said, "I'm not sure that I follow you."

"Nevertheless, when you correct your understanding of time, you will also adjust and correct your misunderstanding of speed and distance. You regard the speed of light as some ultimate speed. Such is the teaching of your twenty-first century pseudoscience. If angels only traveled at the speed of light, they'd be almost as slow as tortoises in getting around the universe."

"What speed *do* you travel at?"

"I travel at the speed of love."

"The speed of love? I never heard of that."

"Most people haven't."

"Is that a measurable rate?"

"Quantifiable, but variable," the gray-eyed man said.

Thrush took up the interrogation. "Mr. E., are you an angel?" she asked eagerly.

"No," he said, smiling once again. "I'm merely an assistant to certain higher powers, though I do possess special areas of expertise."

"A specialist?" Marie asked, "In what?"

"In whatever you need at the moment."

"Our friend Freddy just died, or was killed. And if we don't get out of here soon, the rest of us are likely to die as well."

"Your friend was killed? By whom?"

"We're not certain," Thrush said, "but it was horrible." She shuddered and began to cry again.

At that moment, Nick walked in from the control center. "Who are *you*?" he demanded suspiciously.

"Honey, this is Mr. E. He's come to help us," Marie explained.

"Come from *where*? *How'd* he get here?" His total distrust was evident in his tone.

"That's a long story, honey. The important thing is that he's here to help."

"Can I call you Nick, or should I call you Santa?" asked Mr. E. with a hint of amusement.

"Call me anything you like if you can help."

"Exactly what kind of assistance do you require?"

"I need to get this craft and my crew quickly out of here in order to preserve their lives and their well-being. I need to finish my annual Christmas run, if that is now at all possible, given the events that have transpired. Of course, my friend of many years, Freddy Deere, is now dead and beyond all help."

"Is that all?" said Mr. E.

"Isn't that enough?" said Nick.

"You never thought that any of this might or could happen, did you?"

"Of course not. I certainly didn't *plan* any of this!"

"I'm sure you didn't," said Mr. E. "It sounds to me like you're the victim of unintended consequences, or the collateral consequences of good intentions."

"I guess," said Nick, shrugging his shoulders.

"Nick, have you ever heard the old saying, 'The road to Hell is paved with good intentions'?"

"I seem to have heard that but I don't think I ever really understood it."

"Then grasp its meaning now and be forever healed from the evil consequences of your *good intentions*."

"How do I do that?"

The deep-set grey eyes were focused intently on Nick. "*You* must find the way. Seek and ye shall find. Wake up and seek!"

"Wake up?" asked Nick.

"You're asleep my friend," said Mr. E., "and nothing comes to a sleeper but a dream. Now, take me to your friend."

"You mean you want to see the body, or rather what's left of it?"

"Exactly."

"Nightingale, please open the portal!" Nick commanded.

Freddy's remains, a few yards from the ship, had been covered with a large towel. Mr. E. pulled the towel off and gazed intently at the remains for a few moments. "Lower part of his left leg, the right knee and a pile of ashes. There wasn't much of him left, was there?"

"Not at all," said Nick, beginning to weep silently. "It was the most awful sight I've ever witnessed. He just suddenly exploded into flame! One moment he was all right, the next, his body was vomiting fire in every direction!"

"And you think it was a case of Spontaneous Human Combustion?" asked Mr. E.

"There was no source of ignition whatever. There was no flash point. What else could it have been?"

"It could have been murder, rather cleverly executed. What was he doing before he died?"

"He'd just finished having an argument with a gentleman named D.A., the local Devil's Advocate."

"I'd say he had the argument and D.A. finished it."

"Either way, the man is now a pile of ashes. He is hopelessly, utterly, irrevocably dead."

"I want to meet this D.A.," said Mr. E.

"Personally, I had hoped to never see him again, but I rather imagine that he's not too far away.

"Call him. Call his name out loud. See if you can summon him."

"Why? For heaven's sake, why?" said Nick.

"I want our plans to be announced to *his* boss. The head honcho needs to know what's going on."

"The *head honcho*?"

"Lucifer. Now call D.A."

Nick took a deep breath of the torrid air, then threw back his head and yelled at the top of his lungs, "DEEEEEEE AAAAAAAAY!"

He was just about to repeat the call when Mr. E. stopped him. "Relax. He heard you and he's coming. In fact he's here now."

"You can see him?" Nick asked, because D.A. hadn't spoken.

"Not to mention feel him, and even smell him. Evil has a definite stench."

The insult apparently prompted D.A. to speak, "And who might *you* be?"

"That's *my* business until I decide to tell it. You *really* don't want to know. Just give your boss a message. My friends are tired of your hospitality, so when I leave, I'll be taking them with me. If you, or he, or anyone else gets in the way of that exodus, I promise you there will be hell to pay!"

"Hell to pay! Is that supposed to be a little play on words?" asked D.A., laughing. His laugh had a seriously sinister undertone.

"Take it any way you like," said Mr. E. "And don't make the mistake of thinking you can do to me what you did to Freddy Deere. I have *no* fear of Fire. None! Fire obeys me like a well-trained dog. Don't make me sic my dog on you, D.A.!"

"Who in the hell do you think you are?" demanded D.A, rather imperiously.

"Oh, now you want a résumé and my references? I'll tell you what. There *are* a few people around here you could ask about me. They used to call themselves prophets. The Bible's Book of First Kings Chapter Eighteen speaks of them as the prophets of Ba-al. I had a little run in with them once on Mount Carmel and fire was pivotal. There were only 450 of them and when I finished kicking their butts, they were happy to come to Hell. You find those prophets of Ba-al and ask *them* for my references. Ask them if they've forgotten a man named Elijah. I think they'll tell you that Elijah knew fire better than any man alive or who has ever lived. Now get out of here and take my message to your boss. Give my regards to the prophets of Ba-al and ask *them* if Elijah is a man to be messed with. Scat, while you can, and if I ever see you again, I promise you it will be at your peril!"

D.A. spoke not one more word. A moment later, Mr. E. said, "He's gone and I don't think he'll want to come back. At least not alone. But you never know. Evil can be awfully ignorant, and ignorance can be awfully evil. So we shall see. But for now, let's attend to your friend."

"Mr. E., I really don't want to bury him here or even leave his ashes here. If we're going to try to leave, can't we take him with us?"

"Yes, I agree. I absolutely think he shouldn't be left here under any circumstances but should be returned home. Why don't you call all your people out here and we'll say a few words. Okay?"

"He'd have liked that," Nick said as he placed the big towel once more over the ashes and remains of his dead friend, the late Frederick Rain Deere. A few minutes later, the entire crew was out of the ship, gathered respectfully around what was left of Freddy's body.

"Thrush," Nick said, would you like to conduct some sort of brief service for Freddy? After all, you are the professional minister."

Thrush nervously licked her lips as she considered the invitation to conduct the obsequies. "Yes, but I didn't know the man. You and Marie have known him for years. If anyone can eulogize him, it would be one of you two."

"True," said Nick. "It's just that as much as I loved him, I'd have to think hard to tell you exactly why. His sterling qualities, such as they were, didn't exactly leap out at you. Marie, would you like to eulogize Freddy?"

A weeping and anguished Marie seemed almost as nervous as Thrush. "I'd like to, but like yourself, I'm not sure what made him loveable. My mind says he was a scoundrel of the first rank. That notwithstanding, like yourself, I loved him, in spite of whatever he was if not because of it."

Mr. E. broke in, "It's wonderful that this man was so loved, and that you have spoken your love of him to the universe. That has assisted his healing and restoration."

"What do you mean?" asked Marie. "The man is beyond all healing or restoration. He's dead!"

"That does not place him beyond healing or restoration," said Mr. E.

"The man is now just a small pile of ashes," said Nick.

"Ashes to ashes and dust to dust," said Thrush.

"Those are the words of man, not God," said Mr. E. "God's words were, 'Let there be...' and he spoke all creation into existence."

"Your friend Freddy is a lot more than a pile of ashes." He reached down and with all the panache and flair of a stage magician, swept the towel off the remains of Freddy.

There were no remains. There were no body parts. There were no ashes. There was only a whole and complete Freddy. Fully restored, he lay curled up in the fetal position, apparently sleeping peacefully.

"Freddy," said Mr. E., "wake up. Wake up Freddy, it's time to get up."

"Wake up, Freddy!" Nick bellowed.

Freddy stirred and opened his eyes. "Nick," he said, "what happened? Did I faint or something?"

For the second time in an hour, the whole group was struck dumb, rendered speechless by an unbelievable sight.

"I was feeling so strange," Freddy said, "then everything just went black."

"But you're okay now, right?" asked Mr. E. suggestively.

"I feel fine now. I had some kind of a nightmarish dream which I don't quite recall, but now I'm fine. Who are *you?*"

"A friend."

"He's more than a friend, Freddy. He's a friend and a savior. This man just brought you back to life!" said Nick.

"Wow! I needed resuscitation?" asked Freddy.

"What you needed goes way beyond resuscitation," said Marie. "You were dead. Your body had been utterly ravaged by fire. There was no life left in the fragments that remained. And now, you are whole again. It is beyond miraculous!"

"You're kidding, right? No such thing is possible. Is it?" asked a dazed Freddy.

"We all just witnessed it," said Enoch. He turned to Mr. E. "How did you do that? Who *are* you?"

"Mr. E. is what he said to call him. He told me that he was a specialist," said Marie. "I find his modesty as astounding as his skills. Healing is one of your specialties, isn't it Mr. E.?"

"I've dabbled in a little healing from time to time."

"Well, if you're a *dabbler* in the healing arts, I would guess that you've dabbled from time to time with great success," said Nightingale.

"And if you're not a doctor, but you're some kind of a specialist, I must ask," said Thrush, "what *is* your profession?"

"I'm a man of God," he said very matter-of-factly.

"I sense that you are a man of many talents," said Marie. "What're your other areas of expertise?"

"Well," he said, "I do all right with wind and water, but primarily, fire."

"Fire?" said Nick. "That's why you told D.A. to ask the prophets of Ba-al if they remembered a man named Elijah who had some experience with fire?"

"Prophets of Ba-al?" asked Thrush, moving closer. "A man named Elijah?"

Mr. E. said nothing.

Thrush pressed, "Mr. E., or whoever you are, I ask you plainly, are you now or were you ever known as Elijah the Tishbite?"

"I am he," said Mr. E., humbly bowing his head.

Thrush went limp. Fortunately, she was standing next to Nick, who caught her before she could hit the ground. There was some momentary concern, but when Mr. E. put his hand on her forehead, she revived immediately.

"I was a pretty run-of-the-mill divinity student," she said, "and not the best of Bible scholars. As I recall, the Book of Kings I and Book of Kings II document Elijah's accomplishments rather well."

"They tell some of the story, but not all by any means," said Mr. E. "Anyway, you can't believe everything you read, until and unless you read with spiritual understanding, and spiritual books should always be read with and for spiritual understanding."

"I clearly remember a number of your exploits, such as healing the widow's son after he had died. You did that, didn't you?"

"Yes. He was all she had."

"And on two occasions, you called down the fire of heaven which consumed and destroyed a captain and fifty men who had been sent to pursue and capture you. Did you not?" Thrush asked.

"Sadly, I must admit I did that. You chase Elijah at your own risk. But let's look at the bright side. The third captain and his fifty men asked me for mercy, and at an angel's request it was granted and they were spared. I'm not *all* bad."

"The Second Book of Kings also says that you parted the waters of the Jordan River, so that you and your protégé Elisha walked across as if on dry land. Did you do that? Like Moses parted the Red Sea for the Children of Israel, did you part the Jordan?"

"I was never a strong swimmer, and the Jordan River was wide, deep and cold. You need to understand that kids born and raised in the desert like me and Elisha are seldom strong swimmers. But I was always a great walker, so, yes... I did that."

"And regarding the prophets of Ba-al, the Bible says that before making utter fools of them in a contest regarding Gods and fire, you *mocked* them. Did you do that?"

"The odds were long at 450 to one. Back then, I was a trash-talkin' mammy jammer. You couldn't just *defeat* the opposition, you had to *crush* them! In those days, I loved to talk plenty of trash. Mocked them? Yes ma'am, I did."

"Mr. E., I'm very glad you're on our side," said Thrush.

"I'm on God's side, unlike the thirteen who are approaching. These disciples of darkness come to destroy you and challenge me. They think to do so using the destructive and inimical power of fire. They do not understand fire. They neither know nor understand that fire is a loving and obedient friend of mine. Do not fear the fire of heaven which I will throw down. It will protect you. Even now they come."

"Elijah!" It was the voice of the Devil's Advocate booming in the twilight of Hell.

Mr. E. turned in the direction of the voice. There were twelve hulking, misshapen humanoids staring at him, but D.A. remained invisible.

"Are you still afraid to show yourself, D.A? Invisibility is not anonymity you know. That won't protect or save you!" he announced. "Nor can these demons! I warned you that if we met again it would be at your peril."

"So you said. You're a liar!"

"Did you check my background with the prophets of Ba-al?"

"They're liars too! Not credible!" His voice seemed to reverberate off the very walls of Hell.

"That's the problem with being a liar, D.A. You don't believe anyone. You didn't believe them, you don't believe me. You don't even believe yourself!"

"I believe me, and I believe in the friends I brought along," D.A. said. His voice brimmed with confidence and had the unmistakable air of one who fully expects to be triumphant.

Mr. E. remained humble. "Introduce me to your demon associates. I've not met any nice demons lately."

"Of course," said D.A. "They'll be the last demons you ever meet. Allow me to introduce my friends: Anger, Fear, Lust, Jealousy, Greed, Hatred, Pride, Envy, Gluttony, Sloth, Despair, and Ego. They are extremely powerful, individually and combined. Collectively, they can not be matched!"

"The Devil's Dozen," said Mr. E. "Well, I'm pleased."

"Pleased?" echoed D.A.

"Yes, I'm pleased that this is going to be my one and only encounter with this pathetic pack of mindless, heartless, bi-lateral lobotomized, pseudo-souls you called your friends. Let the festivities begin!" He raised his arms over his head.

"Fire of Heaven, protect the Children of Light!" Elijah cried out, waving his right arm in a big circle. Immediately, a ring of white fire encircled the *Santa Maria* and all the crew.

"As for these others," his raised left arm described a counter clockwise arc in the direction of the demons, "let the hot rains of heavenly justice helter them back to the skelter of oblivion which spawns all evil!"

Suddenly, the dozen demons were encompassed by a ring of black flame. Several of them tried immediately to run and break out of it, but couldn't. The fire line appeared to be an invisible and impenetrable brick wall. Shouting in confusion, they fell back to the center of the circle where they began to whimper.

A few drops of fire appeared to fall within their circle. Then it began to drizzle fire on them. Each drop of fire that pelted them brought an agonizing scream.

They called out for help, "D.A., help us! Do something! We're trapped. Send for Lucifer!"

The molten fire falling from the sky increased in intensity as did their screams and cries for relief. They pleaded for assistance, begging with all their might and main, "Lucifer, save us! Oh, mighty Prince of Darkness, come to our aid!"

The outer ring of encircling black fire began to close in on them. At first, it seemed that the black flames were crackling, as fire often does. Then, it seemed that the flames were not crackling, but were cackling, like a witch or some old crone. Then the fire, burning ever closer and more intensely, actually could be heard laughing!

"Lucifer! HELP! Please, Lucifer! Save us from this madman who has brought Heaven's fire to Hell! D.A! Get Lucifer! Pleeease!!"

One at a time, the deadly black flames seemed to target a victim with laser-like accuracy, dance into the panicked circle, and strike with Antaean force. The molten rain fell relentlessly as the shrieking demons dropped one by one. Only when the last demon had been vaporized by the cosmic fire was there any remission of the black flame and the molten rain.

Mr. E. turned to the crew. They were open-mouthed and wide-eyed, transfixed by the scene of horror and destruction before them. They cowered near the ship. "Are you guys all right?" he asked, trying to be reassuring.

No one was capable of speech, but everyone nodded.

Marie, who had been silently praying all the while, remembered the words of the Ninety-First Psalm: *A thousand shall fall at thy side, and ten thousand at thy right hand; but it shall not come nigh thee. Only with thine eyes shalt thou see and behold the reward of the wicked.*

Mr. E. waved his arm, and the protective flame surrounding them and the ship disappeared. He turned to the smoldering circle where the demons had been consumed. There were no visible remains. The pungent stench of brimstone, burning flesh, and death bore mute testimony to the carnage that had just taken place moments earlier.

Mr. E. cried out in a loud voice. "D.A., I know you're still here. Don't think you've escaped!"

There was no response.

"D.A., I know you're still here. Answer me now or I'll send my fire dog to chew off half of your ass!"

"Yes sir, Mr. Elijah sir!"

"D.A. I'm not finished yet. I'm going to give you another little demonstration of what I can do with fire." He turned to Nick and the crew, "Guys, let's take a little stroll over to the lake of fire. I want you to see something. D.A., you come with us."

The disembodied voice of D.A. responded immediately, "Yes sir, Mr. Elijah, sir."

They walked westward to the shoreline of the fiery lake. Huge roiling waves of flame undulated to and fro like so many dancing girls in a Turkish harem.

"So this is what a lake of fire looks like up close," said Nick.

"Actually, this is an ocean and not a lake," said Mr. E. "But it all works the same. I want D.A. to see what I do here so that he can give his boss an accurate report. Are you paying attention, D.A.?"

"Yes sir, I am."

"It is possible for fire to become so hot that it no longer burns. Allow me to demonstrate. I am going to heat this whole ocean of flame to that point."

He lifted both his arms, and muttered a few words they couldn't hear or understand. He lowered his arms into the flames and began to throw fire on all of them. It didn't burn. It was fire but without any heat. It had no temperature, and gave no sensation of flame. They were astounded.

"Furthermore," he continued, "if I want to change the temperature from that of fire to that of ice, it's easily done." He raised his arms again and muttered a few more words, then turned to them and said, "Have you ever wanted to be a fire eater? Who would like to try a firesicle? I promise you, it's tastier than a popsicle!"

Everybody tried a firesicle and agreed he was right. Eating a firesicle was more fun than eating a popsicle. You didn't have to worry about the drip.

"Of course, fire is so wonderfully malleable, we could easily change it to the consistency of snow and then you could play in it and really have fun!"

He lifted his arms, pronounced a few words, and it was done. The ocean of flame now had the consistency of snow. It looked like fire but if you ate it, it tasted like a snow cone, and you could walk in or on the flames, which Mr. E. promptly did.

Waving his arms, smiling and beckoning, he invited them to join him. "Come on in! The fire is fine!" He splashed around with the wanton joy of a child on holiday. Everyone declined to join him in the flames. The problem was it still *looked* like fire, and that was frightening. As so often happens, human beings perceived danger where there was none.

"What do you think of fire now?" asked Mr. E. rather triumphantly, stepping out of the flames.

"Amazing!" said Enoch.

"Unbelievable!" said Washburn

"Absolutely incredible!" said Thrush.

"I don't believe what I've seen," said Nick.

"D.A.," said Mr. E., "I'm going to leave this ocean of flame in its present condition. You tell Lucifer what happened to it. And tell him that this is nothing compared to what I'll do if I ever have to come back here again. Remind him that ever since he fell from Heaven, angels outnumber demons two to one, and tell him that if I need to come back here I'll bring so many angels with me that this place will never again be the same! Do you understand the message?"

"Yes sir, Mr. Elijah, sir!"

"Good, then see that Lucifer gets it. And know this one thing more: you yourself are now living proof that the infinite mercy of God extends even into Hell. If it didn't you'd have been destroyed this very day along with all your friends. Now go, and may we never meet again."

A moment later, he said, "Good, he's gone."

"How can you tell?" asked Nick.

"Elementary, my friend. Elementary! But now, we need to deal with your problems. Okay? You and yours need to escape from Hell and you need to complete your rounds, is that correct?"

"Absolutely!" said Nick.

"As the Chief Guide told you, Hell has its own rules and laws of physical phenomena. The reason you can't get out of Hell is that you entered through a one-way gate. Therefore while you can gain admittance through that gate, you can't exit through it. It swings one way only."

"But it doesn't affect you?" Enoch asked.

"I operate under a different set of laws," said Mr. E.

"The Second Book of Kings says that the prophet Elijah ascended to Heaven in a chariot of fire drawn by horses of fire and surrounded by a whirlwind which he also seemed to be the master of. Is that true?" asked Thrush.

"Absolutely."

"Unimaginable!" said Nick.

"Imagine this," said Mr. E. "You call Triple A for help and they can't get you started. Then what?"

"They tow you," said Nick, "to wherever you can get help or want the vehicle taken, even if it's back to your house."

"I'm glad Marie had the foresight to phone H.R.A.!"

"H.R.A.?" Marie asked. "What's H.R.A.?"

"Heavenly Roadside Assistance," said Mr. E. "We'll go anywhere to help our members, and today, I think you probably need to be towed back home."

"Are you suggesting what I think?" asked Nick.

"I'm suggesting that my horses of fire and chariot of fire need to tow that unreliable twenty-second century relic back to your compound until you can effect repairs to your hardware and rewrite the software and other programs."

"But I have a delivery schedule to keep!" protested Nick.

"We'll keep that first," said Mr. E. "Then I'll deposit you in that frozen wasteland you call home after we drop off Freddy in Florida."

"We can keep my delivery schedule?" asked Nick. "You mean Santa Claus won't have to disappoint anybody?"

"Not a single solitary soul," said Mr. E.

"That's a huge job, Mr. E. It calls for making an incalculable number of stops and deliveries–"

"Which your incapacitated machinery can not presently make. Not only that, your crew is no longer fresh. They're all stressed."

"Enoch, what do you think?" asked Nick.

"Boss, if the truth be told, I do feel a little... burned out. No pun intended."

"Remember what I told you, Marie. What you think of as sequential moments are all one and the same in God's eternal now. So all the stops that Santa Claus needs to make are really only one and the same stop for me, taking place at the same time in multifarious locations. There's really nothing to it."

"Huh?" asked Nick.

"Your loving wife will explain it to you," said Mr. E. "Right now, I'll summon my horses and chariot of fire and hitch you up for the tow. Okay?"

* * * * *

Twenty-four hours later in the northern fortress.

"Boss," said Enoch, munching on a bon bon, "We need to discuss my new employment and benefits package."

Nick swiveled a bit in his high-backed judge's chair, put his feet up on the desk, and took a small sip of his champagne. "Didn't I tell you we couldn't afford any raises at this time?"

"You did use those words, but that wasn't the bottom line," said Enoch.

"What was the bottom line?"

"You said I could have a raise 'when hell freezes over.' Correct me if I'm wrong, but I believe we've witnessed that."

* * * * *

And that's how Santa Claus survived the holiday season of 2010 and managed to successfully complete his scheduled deliveries with the help of the prophet Elijah. Some may think this an improbable story, but those who can appreciate and fathom the probability of the improbable will be forever blessed as faith supplants their doubt and fears, and rearranges so-called 'reality.'

Happy Holidays forever, and may all the mornings of your life be filled with sunshine.

NO! I said "Off to the SCHMIDT HOUSE"

THE WORST CHRISTMAS WISH LIST ITEM
by Jerry Cole

The worst Christmas gift item I ever put on a list was a used, but mint condition, Lamborghini. It was a fine wish list item until I actually started to think about it. If you know anything about this car, or my financial means, you can probably guess why it was such a terrible gift idea. There is a reason for the "gas guzzler" tax on this car. You can kind of ignore that though, since gas mileage is not actually even a consideration.

Maintenance on this car is a must. (Did you ever hear of a Lamborghini winning or even finishing Le Mans?) In competition, they sometimes last several laps. For me, that would be a few laps around the block. After that, the car would, no doubt, be stuck in the garage, unstartable.

As for the gas, it needs to be driven FAST once in a while I am told; photo radar seems to make this unlikely. If you can find a mechanic, maintenance and repairs are prohibitively expensive. Long story short, the car does not use much gas sitting in the garage.

I am scratching this one off my gift list. I think I will go for a winning lottery number instead. They both have about the same chance of ever happening, but if I win I could afford the Lamborghini and a chauffeur driven Rolls to go visit it at the shop.

Now, I will make it a point not to think about it.

MAMA
by Doris Cohen

About the Author

  Born in Philadelphia, raised in Camden, New Jersey, Doris was married to Bernard Cohen fifty-seven years. A Phoenix resident since 1974, widowed 2006, she has three daughters and two grandsons. Her writing career spans decades: Columnist Woodrow Wilson High School, Camden; Contributor Jr./Sr. High School column, *Philadelphia Evening Bulletin*; Editor teen page Camden community newspaper, *The Voice*; Contributor *Hearing Dealer* magazine; Columnist Cinnaminson, N.J., *Little Paper*; Columnist Phoenix *Valley News*; Op-Ed Commentaries *Arizona Republic* 1999 and 2007; Op-Ed Commentary *East Valley Tribune*; Winner poetry contest *Orange County Register*; Member Writer's Inspiration Group; Contributor *Reminisce* magazine; Member Jerry's Writers Group.

Mama always did her best to "make" Christmas for me, her only child. Although we were a Jewish family, I think she thought I would feel bewildered and hurt if I didn't receive gifts as other children did on Christmas Day. I would probably cry.

I never really experienced Hanukkah because our extended family could not afford gift-giving, especially eight nights in a row as is traditional. Just one aunt and uncle gave me money called Hanukkah gelt. And with that they encouraged me to open a savings account at our local bank. No spending it yet!

This way of saving was known as a Christmas Club. Starting in January customers would place a dollar per week in this special account and by Christmas would have fifty dollars to spend as they pleased. It was a fortune during the Great Depression. There may have been interest accrued that my young mind did not quite understand but would soon learn to appreciate.

What I truly enjoyed at the time were the coin-like gold foil-wrapped chocolate candies that were a substitute for money. Those were given to me by some of my relatives.

As for Mama's efforts, she saw to it that I received the things I wanted from Santa Claus. I believed in him until I was seven and would have continued to believe if it weren't for my twelve-year-old cousin. She told me and her five-year-old brother Santa did not exist. "The presents come from your mother and father," she said, emphatically and with glee.

But at five years old I was thrilled to wake up Christmas morning and find items not under a tree but scattered or hidden throughout the house. There was an easel-type blackboard replete with chalk and an eraser, a wicker doll carriage almost as big as a real one, and a sleek sled for belly flops during the snowy New Jersey winters. Clothes were included in the hunt, but everybody knows kids hate clothes for birthdays and Christmas!

I still have the blackboard and the sled in the garage. The doll carriage is in the guest bedroom and holds the Shirley Temple doll I received the Christmas I was seven. It held each of my three children when they were infants.

That first year we spent living in Phoenix was a busy one. Christmas came even more quickly and seemed so different from the holidays in the Northeast. There was no snow and it was a balmy seventy-two degrees. Inside were gifts lined up on the living room floor. I counted five rows, one for each member of our family, totaling sixty packages. Once again, there was no tree or other substantial evidence of the holiday; just a mixture of small Hanukkah and Christmas decorations.

The family gathered and we began taking turns opening presents. I had pangs of regret. Mama, widowed for several years, was back in New Jersey alone and not yet ready to join us permanently. I noticed a strange pile of gifts in a corner. And where was our oldest daughter? She had slipped out of the house with the car keys, I was told.

We had almost reached the end of the four rows of packages when the front door sprang open. In stepped the missing daughter with Mama! She had been sent an airline ticket by her grown-up and now-working granddaughter.

It was beyond a five-year-old's dreams. Mama was here for the holidays with us.

Sharing the joys of Christmas!

A PHOENIX CHRISTMAS
by Melanie Tighe

The only snow falling is on plasma screens,
as the snowbirds flock to the putting greens.
Wearing shorts in winter, they're easy to spot;
any local can tell you—this ain't hot!
Visa cards swipe-swipe making store owners smile,
as the sun dances cross roofs of red tile.
Strains of *Feliz Navidad* cling to the breeze
and merry lights wrap round trunks of palm trees.
Even the grand saguaro glows in the night,
draped with tacky, strings of blue Christmas light.
We all shake our heads as the weathermen show
the rest of the country pounded by snow.
We shiver as we picture that cold frigid scene,
and watch the snow fall on our plasma screen.

1968: MOONRISE IN MANHATTAN
by Lesley Sudders

About the Author

✒ Lesley left the corporate world for self-employment and time to pursue her lifelong passion for writing—often transforming experiences and people met along the way into fictional narratives in short stories and novels. She believes fiction can be a way to tell a truth about any given subject. A Colorado native, she has lived in Aspen, Denver, San Francisco, and New York, and traveled in the U.S., Mexico, Venezuela, and Europe. Lesley now resides in Phoenix with her husband and writing collaborator, Eduardo Cerviño. They write under the pen names of Les and Ed Brierfield.

Dodging the icy winds blowing off the Hudson River, I hurried along 34th Street. It was Christmas Eve, 1968, and incredibly cold. It didn't help that mini-skirts were in vogue. I was stylish but freezing.

My friend Susan waited for me at her hotel near the Empire State Building. We planned to grab a quick supper, and then walk to a neighborhood theatre to see a highly touted new movie, *2001: A Space Odyssey*.

At the same time, miles overhead, a drama was unfolding. Jules Verne's dream of a man on the moon was one step closer to realization.

"It's great to see you," I said to Susan, an old friend from home, as I hugged her.

"You too. My, you look all sophisticated and big-city. I feel sort of like a hick." She was being coy.

"A Jewish princess like you? I don't think so. But you do look warm." She was sensibly wearing pants with her heavy coat.

As we left the warm lobby of Susan's hotel, the shock of the cold made us shiver.

"Man, I thought Denver was cold, but this is completely different. It did not seem this cold when I got in this afternoon," she exclaimed.

"Yes, the humidity makes it feel worse. I'm getting used to it. Want to get a cab?"

"No, I'm okay if you are. Let's go eat."

We went to Horowitz's Deli. The place was not expensive and the food was good—hearty soups and big sandwiches, mostly.

"Well, happy holidays," I said. "This year I don't have the money or time off to go home for Christmas. I really appreciate your company." I toasted her with my tea.

She toasted back. "Since Chanukah was over a few days ago, this little trip worked out well. I'll see my aunt and uncle in Boston before I head home." She stopped to take a few bites of mushroom soup before continuing, "So how long have you been in New York? I can't quite remember."

"I came in May. Although I hope to get an apartment soon, I still live in the women's residence club. Most of the other women are youngish, my age more or less. The place is clean, cheap, and well located, and I've made friends there."

"You mentioned you got a job rather easily. Do you like it?" she asked.

"Yes, I do. It's at an architectural firm and we are really busy. An interesting place, kind of cosmopolitan. The staff is about a hundred people from many parts of the world."

"Some of them eligible men, I would suspect," she said, with a gleam in her eye.

"Oh, yes. Indeed. But nothing to talk about so far." I shrugged.

"It sounds like things are going okay for you."

"Yes, for me personally. New York is exciting and I am enjoying it in general." I chewed my lip for a moment instead of my sandwich.

"But…?" she said.

"It seems almost irresponsible or uncaring to enjoy things too much, when you think about all the problems. It has been a terrible year in so many ways. It's numbing, the constant news about Viet Nam or civil rights tensions. I mean, this whole year has been so turbulent. Although I don't do drugs, sometimes I understand why it may seem a good escape. It's hard to know what one can do," I said, somewhat dejectedly.

"Yes, I understand. I can hardly watch television. You remember my friend Jan?" Susan asked. "Her husband is at the army hospital in Denver, the amputee ward. He lost one leg in Viet Nam. I visit him when I can."

I nodded.

Mrs. Horowitz's pastrami sandwiches and homemade pickles were delicious. We ate quietly for a moment.

"Were you still in Denver when Dr. Martin Luther King was assassinated?" Susan asked.

"Yes. That night I was cashiering at the dining room of the Rockies Hotel, downtown. Most peopled cancelled their dinner reservations as there was some fear about rioting around town, but nothing much happened. His death was shocking."

"Yes, I remember. It was in April. I was at home with my sister," said Susan.

"Then in June, just after I arrived here, Robert Kennedy was assassinated. I awoke to that news, sat on the edge of my bed, and cried. I felt sadness for the whole country." I paused, remembering. "A few days later, his body lay in state in St. Patrick's Cathedral, a few blocks from my office. I imagined I could drop by on my lunch hour to pay my respects. Ha!"

She glanced up, a questioning look on her face.

"By nine in the morning, people were lined up six or more abreast and streaming down the street. They formed a quiet and orderly procession that went on all day. I could see this from my office window, the closest I was able to get."

I paused again to collect my thoughts. "The following Saturday, I knew they would transport his body from New York to Washington by rail from Pennsylvania Station. The same day, I went to visit a friend in Philadelphia, but I knew enough to get to the station early: six in the morning. As we rolled along, I saw people gathering near the tracks wherever they could, all the way from New York to Philadelphia. I assumed it would be like that all the way to D.C. It was very moving, and–"

Susan interrupted, "I imagine it was. Then, a few months later, it was awful seeing the Chicago police and the National Guard roughing up American citizens at the Democratic National Convention, didn't you think?"

"Of course." We finished our sandwiches and declined the waiter's suggestion of dessert.

"Well, this has been cheerful," she said as she folded her napkin. "So what do you do for fun?" she asked, in a lighter tone.

"Sorry to let the conversation take a somber turn. Yes, fun. I visit the museums, go to Broadway plays, Lincoln Center, and walk in the park when it's warmer; of course, there is no shortage of shops and restaurants. We will do some of those things while you are here. It's just a matter of choice. And money, and maybe the weather."

"I'd especially enjoy seeing the Museum of Modern Art."

I nodded, saying, "I love it. And the Metropolitan Museum. If I live here a hundred years, I don't think I could see it all. However, this reminds me of a happy event. A few weeks ago, I was at the Metropolitan. I caught the bus going down Fifth Avenue to go home. A few blocks later, there was a delay in traffic, and we could see Richard and Pat Nixon leaving their apartment to go to the wedding of their daughter Julie to David Eisenhower. Julie was quoted as saying that they didn't want to be married after the Nixons moved to the White House, as she and David were 'historic enough' or something like that.

"The bus stopped at 57th Street, as the Secret Service had barricaded Fifth Avenue. I decided to walk home from there. By the way, walking around the city is one of my favorite modes of entertainment. I love the street life—it's so vibrant."

She grinned. I knew she too enjoyed strolling around.

"Anyway, the wedding was to be held at the church of Dr. Norman Vincent Peale, not far from where I live. As I neared it, the crowds increased, and I saw some women from my residence club. We watched the newlyweds emerge and get into their limo. Weddings are always fun, I think. Or at least I hope so."

I glanced at my watch, and the waiter brought our check. Fortified, we stepped outside to brave the cold for the short walk to the movie theater.

That movie, *2001*, was amazing, not easy to understand, and unlike anything I had ever seen. The special effects were mind-blowing, to use a relatively new expression from the rampant drug culture.

Susan and I left the theater somewhat speechless. As we walked along the avenue to my place, no one on the street near the theater spoke, as if doing so would break the mood.

For a moment, the cold, clear Christmas night reminded me of magical times in my childhood with my family in the mountains of Western Colorado.

Back at the residence club, some other young women gathered with us in the club's kitchenette and we brewed hot tea. Someone switched on a radio.

That evening, Apollo 8, the first manned mission to the moon, had entered lunar orbit. The astronauts—Frank Borman, Jim Lovell, and William Anders—were broadcasting live from space. We did not have access to television, but it wasn't needed. My imagination, fueled by the marvelous movie I had just seen, provided the images.

"The vast loneliness is awe-inspiring," Lovell said, "and it makes you realize just what you have back there on Earth."

They ended the broadcast with the crew reading from the Book of Genesis. William Anders began by saying, "For all the people on Earth, the crew of Apollo 8 has a message we would like to send you.

> *In the beginning God created the heaven and the earth.*
> *And the earth was without form, and void; and darkness was upon the face of the deep.*
> *And the Spirit of God moved upon the face of the waters. And God said, Let there be light: and there was light.*
> *And God saw the light, that it was good: and God divided the light from the darkness.*

Jim Lovell read the next part, and Frank Borman finished the recitation. He then added, "And from the crew of Apollo 8, we close with good night, good luck, a Merry Christmas, and God bless all of you—all of you on the good Earth."

Tears filled my eyes. The tragedies of the year receded in my mind. The ancient text had reminded me that in spite of the ugly things humans do to each other and the planet, our world was good. A feeling of hopefulness I realized had been absent throughout the year reappeared and my spirit felt reenergized.

Susan, the other girls, and I walked to the nearest window and gazed up at the moon as if we could see the little spaceship. Susan said, "There is a man in the moon, after all. Can you imagine that?"

I knew Jules Verne was smiling, somewhere.

HEAVENLY STAR
by Richard Oppman

I looked to the heavens and asked for a sign.
A shooting star was all I could find.
I met the lady the one of my dreams.
She loves another or so it would seem.
I looked in her eyes I longed for a kiss.
My heart fell for her in wanton bliss.
My shooting star is gone in the night.
She touched my heart on her heavenly flight.
I miss her now all I have is time.
I look to the heavens and ask for a sign.

SOLSTICE 2090
by Jerry Cole

About the Author

✒ W. Jerald "Jerry" Cole has had a desire to write speculative fiction since he was in college. Life intervened. Since then he raised a family, has a wife and grown sons and is now retired, working on his writing. Over the years, doing everything from plumbing to Information Technology, he has had plenty of opportunity for technical and business writing but, except for note taking on the bus, he was too busy for his fiction. He now finally has time to work on his writing. He is involved with a local writers group and is transcribing his thirty years of notes to use on several short story and novel ideas.

Daddy says we are going to do something that decades ago they used to do around the time of the solstice. We don't really think much about the solstice these days. They explained it to us at school, but we learn a lot of stuff at school that doesn't seem like it matters. At least I knew what Daddy was talking about when he mentioned it at the dinner table.

When I asked why we were going to do this, we got into a lengthy discussion about "nostalgia," celebrating reunions with relatives and stuff like that. He explained there used to be scads of things people did around the solstice, just because of nostalgia. They even had holidays around the solstice. Most used some religious justification, but they could still all be classified as solstice holidays, because of their timing. Basically, the activity was to stir good memories about times past, and maybe restart some traditions. Daddy laughingly mentioned there once being a song about what we would do— although it was not exactly going to be "over the river and through the woods;" more like "under the ocean and through the woods." He said we might even see some snow on our way to visit grandma, who is stationed at the Highpoint Observatory.

When your home is hundreds of feet below the surface of the ocean, you do not see much snow. You don't go out "stargazing." You don't really notice days getting longer, or shorter. With this journey topside we might get to do some of these things.

Daddy says they used to call this time of year Christmas. He didn't say where that name came from. I asked, but as he often does, he said, "Look it up." Mom says he does that because he is a lazy teacher, but Daddy says the best way to learn is by knowing how to teach yourself.

Daddy teaches, but mostly he is a scientist, so he gets to go up to the surface a lot. He even brought us down some fruit and vegetables to try a couple of times. To me they tasted much better than the ones grown in our hydroponics garden. He believes someday everyone will be able to go up there, as they used to. He likes to talk about this. Mom says it is his passion. Maybe that is why his science specialties are climatology and meteorology.

He hasn't said anything to us kids, but I have heard him talking to others: Things seem to be getting better topside. The climate is cooling. Ice caps are reforming. Winters are much like they were a hundred years ago. Some people from Atlantis II might move up there to live soon.

Daddy has told us Atlantis II was just an experimental habitat. It was not designed to be self-sustaining this long. Electricity was a big problem. Even a nuclear power plant needs to be refueled. Food, water, and air were handled well in the design, but over the years, with great effort, some redundancy was added. Cooperation among the surviving population areas was essential. There were dangerous salvage expeditions to some of the abandoned cities and their factories as well. Daddy added, "In a way, Atlantis II has been hanging on for decades. The populace has been wondering if there will be a day that we could move back to the surface."

Daddy rigged up our trip as a professional experiment. (He says that just means his bosses agreed to make it part of his job.) Atlantis II has one road to the top, although it is more like a big pipe than a road. Some people call it a giant snorkel or just The Snorkel. It took a twenty-five year project to build it. The Snorkel acts as a conduit for electrical power from the solar and wind generation facilities on the surface. It also pulls down fresh air from the surface, filtering it with ocean water.

We spent several days gathering gear and packing for the trip. An e-jeep is pretty small, but we were only going up for a couple of days (depending on weather). Still, we had to bring all kinds of special clothing and stuff. Daddy says there never was any climate control topside.

Finally the day came. We all stuffed ourselves into the vehicle. Mommy and Daddy sat in front, while Billy and I sat in back. Billy is ten and I get to be called his big sister, at twelve, but he just finished a growth spurt and is taller than me.

Daddy's boss was there, along with Aunt Amal and Uncle Habib, to wave us good-bye. Everybody seemed excited. Billy and I became even more excited because of it and were hardly able to keep quiet or be still. Once we staged our way through the air-lock to The Snorkel everything got noticeably quieter.

Daddy explained some stuff about The Snorkel. It isn't one giant pipe these days. It is subdivided to provide redundancy. We wouldn't want a leak to keep us from getting supplies or air in Atlantis II. Part of it is used for air intake, with the air moving from chamber to chamber with assistance of some compressors. At the bottom the air gets pulled through water to filter it before it is let into the habitat. The part we are in usually has the airlocks on the ends closed, and that one is designed for the e-jeeps to use.

I had never been in an e-jeep before. Atlantis II is small enough that powered vehicles only get used for hauling stuff around the habitat. I never realized how powerful they were. Daddy made us get out and walk when Billy and I started fussing in the back seat. It didn't take long to realize we were going up a pretty steep grade in this part of The Snorkel, and it was a heck of a lot easier to ride than walk it. About the second time we stopped to catch our breath Daddy let us back in and asked us what we learned. Daddy always likes multiple answers: one, two, three. First we learned not to fuss so much that we annoyed Mommy and Daddy. Second, we learned that walking up The Snorkel was more like climbing than walking. Third, we learned that we sure did prefer riding in the e-jeep. I even had a fourth lesson; Daddy would say I extrapolated. I learned I sure was glad e-jeeps never seem to break down.

The Atlantis II habitat is a couple of miles out in the ocean. The trip up would not only take us to shore and to the ocean surface, but would continue far past shore, up the slope, beyond the dangers of tides and flood waters. As we continued our long ride, Daddy started talking about his passion. He is big on starting from the beginning, so we got a little history lesson first. He told us how warnings about the possible effects of global warming had not been exaggerated. Eventually, weather extremes and rising ocean levels made coastline cities uninhabitable. There went forty percent of the population, looking for elsewhere to live. Most never found it.

Extremes in weather were tough on humans. There had always been blizzards, tornadoes, and hurricanes, but they became more frequent and much more severe. Places flooded that had never flooded before. Winds were too strong for most of the standard construction of the time. Shingles became deadly missiles. Frame houses were turned into kindling. Skyscrapers became windowless skeletons. Dams overflowed and collapsed. Most roads and bridges became unusable.

Daddy says people have to overcome a lot of social inertia before they start adapting to reality. Most people didn't adapt quickly enough. Once the weather extremes started destroying infrastructure everything went wrong. Uncontrolled fires, floods, disease, starvation. It all happened.

Amidst all the chaos, somebody liberated a bunch of secret stuff, locked away by governments and big corporations around the world. Lots of it got distributed over the Internet before it died. This helped some (isolated government and corporate strongholds) keep things together long enough to actually get people launched into space. The moon acted as another launch point, as hibernating people got sent off to other planets and solar systems. Nobody knows if any of them woke up and survived. Daddy told us, "At least all the eggs were not in the same basket anymore."

After the great planetary exodus, the few humans staying on Earth had to survive by extraordinary means. There were places underground, underwater, and even a few strongly built habitats on the surface of the planet. But now the world population was measured in thousands, not billions.

Periodically we stopped to stretch and use the facilities. The designers of The Snorkel originally built rest areas for the workers who were building it. For safety reasons, each rest area was a pressurized chamber with air-locks to the tunnel, and to the water. Daddy said there was only one big accident during construction, and it was near the surface. The workers escaped a pressurized chamber through a water-side hatch using a floating capsule. Their floating life-boat, really a giant balloon, was picked up by a boat from Atlantis II in a rescue aided by a rare break in the weather. The accident proved that the safety valves on the snorkel worked as designed.

Daddy announced our location as we passed the sea-level marker. Inside the snorkel, it all looked pretty much the same. He continued telling us about how life used to be on the surface. He talked about things like wind and rain, and snow. I got rain. Heck, I take showers all the time. But snow, that just didn't make sense to me. I had seen pictures and videos of it, but it seemed kind of make-believe to me, like special effects in an old movie.

He told us how there used to be so many people that the earth and the ocean could hardly feed them all. He explained how there were problems catching enough edible fish and shellfish to eat. How could that be? Today the harvesters have no problem keeping us fed in Atlantis II. Daddy says the planet tends to repair itself, given the chance.

After Daddy finally stopped talking, I think I must have dozed off for a while, hypnotized by the humming of the e-jeep's motors. I was startled when we lurched to a stop and Mommy performed her sing-song "rise and shine" routine to wake us up.

"Last stop before we are outside on the shore," Daddy announced. He may get up here all the time, but he sure seemed excited about it. It was time to bundle up in all those special clothes we had brought. Only this last air-lock separated us from the weather.

Outside it was cold, cloudy, and windy. Our exit from The Snorkel came out on the top of a hill, so we were really feeling the wind. It blew so hard I could hardly hear myself think. One part of the snorkel projects way up in the air; a half cylinder tower going up about a hundred feet. For some reason there is a flashing red light at the top.

Daddy quickly directed the e-jeep to the trail we would be following. He called it a road, but it sure didn't look like any of the nice smooth roads we had in Atlantis II. We could see some of the experimental gardens scattered nearby. Daddy pointed out the one where those tasty vegetables and fruit were picked for us earlier in the year.

When we came to a sheltered spot, protected by trees, we stopped and Dad deployed the canopy and side-curtains on the e-jeep. It was still noisy, but at least we could hear each other talk now without resorting to the radio equipped helmets we brought. (Daddy is big on the "be prepared" thing.)

The e-jeep continued up the trail, easily navigating the changes in grade, wash-outs, and other obstacles that presented themselves thanks to its hydrogen fuel-cell powering an electric motor on each wheel. Daddy said the e-jeeps were designed for this kind of use, long before they ever used them in Atlantis II. Somebody decided the jeeps from World War II were a good idea, better than the electric or Eco-Safe ATVs built just after the turn of the century. When they combined ideas they ended up with the e-jeep.

After a while I decided to see if Daddy had anything to add to the stuff I had learned about solstice holidays. I told him I had looked it up, but didn't understand some of the references to religious holidays. I read much of what he already told me about Christmas, that it wasn't the only holiday they celebrated, and that there were holidays around solstice time long before there was ever a Christmas. But I didn't really understand the significance of it.

Daddy went into teacher mode. He explained about equinoxes, and how they helped people know when to plant and harvest. Astronomy was important to people before they had sciences. Sometimes they paid attention for practical reasons. People were kind of superstitious, or religious, and tied significance to constants like the patterns they observed in the sky, changes in the lengths of days, solstice.

I had to think about that for a while. It felt like one of Daddy's stories where he withholds his point, hoping you will get it before he announces it.

The e-jeep may have been reliable and powerful, but it sure wasn't much for heat, even with the canopy and side curtains sheltering us. Despite the special warm clothes Daddy made us put on, I could feel the cold trying to sneak in around my wrists and neck. I could feel the cold every time I took a breath. It felt like it was trying to steal my warmth every way it could.

When I exhaled, I saw my breath in the air; it reminded me of the first time I had seen that. It was in a walk-in freezer doing my service time putting some freshly caught and cleaned fish away for long-term storage.

How could people live in this?

Daddy clarified; it wasn't cold all year. People built shelters and used fires to protect themselves from the cold of winter. Of course, closer to the Equator they didn't worry about it so much.

As the e-jeep trail left the protection of the forest and went up on a ridge for a ways, the wind buffeted us quite a bit. Pieces of white stuff bounced off the windows and the hood as they flew past. It became so thick that we could hardly see ahead. When the trail led us down into a more sheltered area Daddy stopped and had us get outside for a break. The cumbersome cold wear made it difficult.

The white stuff was really coming down now, but the wind was almost stopped. The white stuff looked different, almost like feathers fluttering down through the sky instead of the white little pellets that had been attacking us earlier. Then it finally clicked in my head. This was snow!

Daddy saw the awestricken expressions on everyone's faces at their first experience with snow. "Thirty years ago you would never have gotten topside to see this. Hold out your hand and catch one in your glove," he said. He paused while we tried and finally succeeded. "Then look real close at it."

As we peered closely Daddy pointed his flashlight at our hands so we could see better. Memories of old school lessons came back to me. This was a snow flake; six points and some incredible geometric tricks in between. Daddy pulled a magnifying glass from a pocket, and held it for us to look at a few of them. Sure enough, each one seemed a little different. I looked at all the flakes tumbling down, and wondered if each one really was different from every other. It made me feel kind of funny as I watched the snow quietly drop from the heavens. Some of the flakes fell, quickly melting on my face. I don't know why, but I opened my mouth to catch one and felt the tiny tingly cold spot on my tongue. I smiled at my success and laughed.

It was all so amazing. My smile kind of got stuck on my face for quite a while, even as Daddy had us all get back in the e-jeep to continue our trip. The ride up took a long time. E-jeeps are strong and reliable, but not very fast, especially under these rough trail conditions. I almost could have walked faster. Billy was sleeping, and I was half asleep myself.

It was dark, the wind had died down, and it was no longer snowing. When we got up to the doorway of the observatory, Daddy turned off the e-jeep lights. They don't like lights on up here by the observatory.

Daddy had us all clamber out and look at the now clear sky. Wow! This was totally different from when you looked up in a planetarium, but that was the only place you kind of got to look at the sky in Atlantis II. In the habitat you get to look outside, but you cannot see far, even in the daytime. You get to see lots of fish and sea creatures, and the vegetation looked much livelier than what we had seen from the e-jeep as we climbed to the observatory.

But looking up at the sky… It seemed so huge. High on the hill, with the horizon hidden by the darkness, if you stared at it you felt like you were going to fall into it. I told Daddy that. Of course he had an answer. "It is more 3-D. The parallax of your vision adds the dimension you don't get from a projection on a dome." As usual, when I asked what parallax meant he told me to look it up.

We all stood there staring at the amazing clear sky. It crossed my mind that the days ahead would be getting longer and longer now. After everything we had squeezed into this day; that seemed wondrous to me.

My imagination spun a scene of what it must have been like living on the surface in ancient times; short cold days, and even colder nights.

Daddy saw the look on my face, and decided it was a good time to finish the story he had cut short earlier.

"When you think about it," he said in his here-comes-the-punch-line tone, "for thousands of years people have looked to the skies. Long before there was civilization and clocks they would judge the time and Earth's season by what they saw above. Some people even thought they could foretell the future by the positions of the stars."

"Imagine seeing warm days and plentiful food disappearing into the face of winter. Life-forms like birds, insects, and many of the mammals migrated or hibernated, leaving the world a starker place. Then think about what it meant to people when they counted the days, measuring their supplies, their survival, life in general, against the progress of the skies."

"Winter weather is far from over during the solstice. But its end is predicted by the astronomical event. There is one word that sums up how people would feel as they saw the days start to become longer."

"Hope."

A FONDNESS FOR FAMILY
by Doris Cohen

The holiday was so special when Aunt Rose and Uncle Al came to visit us on Christmas morning. We always enjoyed their company whether they had been invited or had simply dropped in. But on Christmas I made it a point that they should come for breakfast and have pancakes with us.

Uncle Al would always bring packages of chewing gum for our three children. Aunt Rose brought beautiful name-brand clothing for our brood who were like grandchildren to her.

I can still picture Uncle Al who preferred to stand rather than sit. His shoes, whether new or old, were so highly polished you could see your reflection in them.

Rose and Al's conversations were always animated and easy to listen to. We learned what was going on with our large, extended family, and the bits of gossip were harmless.

Yes, they were a very special aunt and uncle who came from both sides of my family. Aunt Rose was my mother's sister and she had married my father's brother. I called them my "double" aunt and uncle. Their son David, an only child, had enlisted in the Navy. He was like a brother to me; I'm sure the same blood flowed through our veins.

The wonderful gifts for my children on Christmas and on their birthdays continued until Rose and Al had grandchildren of their own. I fully understood this and never became resentful. Aunt Rose and Uncle Al enjoyed my family during their "little" years and eventually turned their attention to their own three grand-tykes.

If only they had lived to know and love the six great-grandchildren who in time came along. Right now and from afar, I merely appreciate photos of the group. If I could, I would be as generous toward them as their great-grandparents had been to my children. Meanwhile, I send concern and love.

REINDEER
by Eduardo Cerviño

Balancing on top of the steel rail of the railroad tracks, I glided forward like a tightrope acrobat. The old bridge over the river lay ahead, and crossing it was the thrilling part of my hike. I was eight years old.

Through the cracks between the ties, I could see the green water below, and a mild sense of danger increased the adventurous feeling of my morning walk.

Midway across the bridge span, the soles of my feet sensed the quivering of an approaching passenger train. It went by once a day and was not due for another hour. The bell from the church spire began to toll, calling parishioners to Sunday mass. This made me realize it was later than I thought. Alarmed but not yet scared, I hurried forward. The vibration from the rail was climbing up my legs. I stepped down from the rail onto the ties and hurried, but there was no time to reach the other end. A high-pitched whistle pierced the air. The train was closer behind the curve than I expected.

My stomach filled with butterflies. My mom would whip my ass if she ever knew. Mother had warned me a dozen times about the trains, but she could do little about my fascination with them.

I was on my way to the opposite shore of the river. There, instead of going to church and listening to soporific sermons, my friend Bernie and I met every Sunday to watch the barges go by or wave at the rushing train.

I have to get out of here, I thought. The train was still beyond the bend, when at the end of the bridge, I saw him walking into the path of the oncoming locomotive, proudly displaying his colossal antlers.

We stared at each other, and what was about to happen erased my own worries.

"Go! Go! Get out of there," I yelled and flapped my arms.

He arched his neck, raised his head, and froze in place. His ears pointed in my direction. The silvery gray fur of his muscular body shone under the morning sun, and his eyes denoted a magical intelligence. His nose—what a sight—his fleshy red nose glowed.

Rolling down the rails with overwhelming power, the diesel engine came into view. I jumped to the side of the bridge, aware of how precariously close to me the train would pass. Embracing a bridge post, I turned my back to avoid looking at it. The structure trembled, the noise was deafening, and my mom appeared in my mind. I thought about the reindeer, fear made me cry, and I promised never to disobey my mom again—all this in a flashing second.

I felt myself being pulled by the collar of my jacket, so strongly that I had to let go of the bridge. I thought the passing train was sucking me along, but miraculously, I was ascending over the river in absolute silence, higher than the bell tower, the tallest structure in town. Below my dangling feet, the bridge and train were getting smaller. I could see my house and my father's boat in the front yard.

My winter jacket felt tight, suspended as I was by its collar. I turned my head around, and there was the reindeer's head, holding my new parka in his mouth.

It's going to tear. Mom is going to get mad, I thought. However, it was wonderful to sashay in the air, and it was colder at this altitude. "Hey! Can you take me down?"

"Where would you like to go?" he answered, but as he began to talk, he let go of me. I plummeted toward the ground, bellowing at the top of my lungs. He dove faster than I could blink and grabbed my parka again. This time I heard the cloth tearing.

"Sorry, it was unintentional," he said, between his teeth.

"It's okay; please don't talk any more," I said. "Just let me down, please."

I saw my friend Bernard on the riverbank, and asked to be taken there; we landed like feathers in the breeze. Bernard's jaw dropped but he said nothing.

"He can talk," I volunteered, pointing at the reindeer. Bernard remained silent. "And he saved me from the train, Bernie." Not a word. "Come here. I think he will let you touch him."

Bernard moved closer with halting steps and wide eyes. "What is his name, Peter?" he finally asked, but I didn't have time to answer.

"I'm Rudolph, the reindeer."

Bernard took two steps back and his coffee-colored face froze.

"My mom has mentioned you," I said. "I can't believe you are here. Do you know who Rudolph is, Bernie?"

"Nope, but he is pretty. Never seen nothing like him."

"Come on; everybody has seen pictures of Santa Claus, right? Rudolph works with Santa."

"Peter," said Rudolph, "Bernard's is one of those houses where the old man has not made toy deliveries in a while."

"Why not? Bernie is my friend, and all my other friends get toys, like me."

Bernard's face was solemn. He began stroking Rudolph's massive neck, but the smile had gone from his face. "It's okay, Peter," he said softly. "Most of my friends this side of the river don't get none of them toys either."

I looked at Rudolph, waiting for an explanation; he lowered his head to my height, and I detected some remorse as he spoke.

"Peter… sometimes it's hard to understand why things are the way they are. Even Santa has economic problems these days, and the light elves run out of time to make packages for every kid."

"Light elves? What are those?" asked Bernard.

"Little, good, magical dwarves who live at the North Pole as Santa's employees. During the year, they walk in the streets all over the world buying things for Santa."

"Don't they make the toys?"

"They used to, but times have changed; these days, 'Santa's, Inc.' is a packaging and distribution center only."

"The stores are full of toys. Why don't they buy some for Bernie?"

"People's donations are down, and there is not enough money to buy toys for every child in the world."

"But what happened with Bernie?"

"Years ago when he was two years old, we ran out of gifts before we got to his side of the river. He is on the old man's list every year; but there are more names on the list of kids younger than him and they have priority. As kids grow older, the dark elves make them stop believing in Santa, so Santa disappears from their lives."

"The dark elves?" asked Bernard.

"Yes, Bernie, bad little monsters who live underground and sabotage Santa's shop, stealing or breaking toys. And what is worse, they visit older kids and whisper in their ears, 'Santa is not real, Santa doesn't exist.' It's terribly frustrating," explained Rudolph.

"What a crock. On the side of the river where I live," said Bernard, "the boys in the 'hood would have punched the daylights out of the dark elves and kicked their asses to kingdom come. Why don't you?"

Rudolph seemed utterly offended. "That's not possible! 'Santa's, Inc.' is a loving enterprise, and we do not approve of violence."

"Bunch of suckers, that's what you are," said Bernard. "Anyway, what is a reindeer like you doing in this part of the woods? You are lucky Bubba is not around; it's hunting season, you know?"

"I'm on vacation with the rest of the team. I stopped to help Peter out of his pickle. Just a coincidence that I am a train watcher and was close by."

"How many of you are around here now?" I asked.

"Eight others. When the train rolls by we let the passengers see us. It makes them happy."

There was a lull in the conversation and I kept thinking of Santa's difficulties. An idea came to my mind, but I needed to consult with my friend Bernie. "Can you wait a minute, Rudolph?" I pulled Bernie aside to talk. He was delighted to hear what I had to say, and we came back to where Rudolph waited.

"Hey! Rudy. Have you seen the movie *The Magnificent Eight*?" I asked.

EDUARDO CERVIÑO

"I believe it is *The Magnificent Seven*, Peter, not eight," said Rudolph.

"Oh, you wuss," said Bernie. "Who is counting?"

"Can you and the rest of the herd meet with us again here tomorrow? Bernie and I have to talk with our baseball team. We are going to help Santa."

Rudolph's nose brightened. "What could be more appropriate than children helping the old man?" he said.

"Tell me: how come you guys can fly and other deer can't?" I asked.

"The old man would fire me if I tell you, and I have a wife and one Rudolpfito to support. Sorry, I can't tell you."

"Look, I promise not to tell anyone, cross my heart and hope to die."

Rudolph thought for a second. "Okay, but all I can say is that it has something to do with flatulence."

"What is that?" asked Bernard.

"You will find out," responded Rudolph. "I'll see you tomorrow."

That afternoon, Bernie and I called a meeting in our tree house. Our baseball team, "The Garden Snakes," had a fearless reputation and we agreed to undertake the mission.

We gathered the next day by the riverbank, and Rudolph introduced the rest of the herd. "These are Dasher and Dancer, Prancer and Vixen, Comet and Cupid, with Donner and Blitzen."

"So including you there are nine reindeer, not eight. Can't you count, compadre?" I said.

"I'm the boss. I don't count myself as one of the team. I don't pull the sleigh; I just point the way."

"As if we haven't noticed," murmured Dancer in Prancer's ear.

"What did you say?" asked Rudolph sternly.

"Nothing, boss, nothing at all," responded Dancer.

"Bastard," whispered Prancer. "If it were not because of the reindeer union, the old man would fire him for not pulling his weight."

I introduced our team of eight players, six boys and two girls. "I'm Peter, these are Paul and Pablo, and these are Bobby, Bernie, and Billy. The girls are Bonnie and Rosita. We brought what we need to deal with the dark elves. We are ready to go, but are worried about our parents."

"We can solve that with magic," said Rudolph. "The same way nobody notices the old man coming down the chimney, your parents will not notice you are gone until you return."

"Then let's go kick some ass," said Bernie.

"Would you please mind your vocabulary," exclaimed Cupid. "Dancer over here is my bottom lady."

Each one of us jumped on a reindeer's back and held tightly to the antlers. Rudolph had no rider. Their bellies swelled, and we floated off the ground in sleigh-pulling formation. At the proper altitude, for safe flying below commercial traffic, the reindeer farted and we took off like rockets.

"Is this the way Santa goes around the world so fast?" I asked Rudolph who was at my side without a rider.

"Yes, Peter; however, with his contribution to the propulsion system, we go even faster than we do now."

The magic of the system was undeniable. If my recollection is correct, we reached 'Santa's, Inc.' almost immediately, leaving behind an odoriferous contrail. The reindeer descended into a desolate spot; there was nothing to see for miles around, save for the immaculate expanse of snow and ice. My friends and I felt the sharpness of the wind on our cheeks and looked at each other for moral support. This was not what we expected to find; there was nothing comforting at the North Pole, except the aroma of hot cinnamon-chocolate brew.

"He is taking a break. I smell it," said Blitzen with his German accent.

"Who? Is it lunch time already?" I asked.

"It doesn't matter. Santa works one hour in the morning and takes a long break the rest of the day. The elves do all the work around here."

"Where?" I asked.

EDUARDO CERVIÑO

A spot in the distance began to glow. The intensity grew steadily, and slowly an enormous igloo became distinguishable from the rest of the icy surroundings. The tunnel entrance opened. It was big enough to let the reindeer and us enter as a group, and then it closed behind us.

The interior light dimmed, and I assumed that with the change of intensity, the igloo might have become invisible from the outside as before.

A village was built inside a bowl-like depression of the terrain; green and flowery gardens surrounded a few dozen gingerbread hostels and barns with redwood tiled roofs. Colorful gift packages of all sizes were piled everywhere—thousands, millions of them, on porches and patios, along the sidewalk, on balconies, and even around the stalls where the reindeer lived. The light elves hummed as they went about their business, giving the narrow streets the festive atmosphere of a carnival in Rio.

Sadly, many of the packages were ripped open, and the broken contents strewn on the ground.

"That's the damage done by the dark elves; it breaks my heart," said Rudolph.

"I hope you had a good time, Cupid," I heard a seductive voice saying and I turned around.

"She likes me a lot," said Cupid, with the droopy eyes of a reindeer in love.

"Who is she?" asked Bernie.

"She is Mary Christmas, Mrs. Claus, from Copenhagen," said Rudolph. "The old man is gaga over her; she is the reason for his long breaks and religious fervor."

"Does Santa go to church a lot?" asked Rosita.

"No, but their bedroom is above the stable, and I can hear them praying every night, yelling, 'Oh my God' over and over," said Rudolph.

"When we go back home, I will tell Mom and the milkman that they are not the only ones who like to pray in the bedroom," said Bernie.

In her red mini-skirt with white fur fringes, and a blouse showcasing her firm and hilly breasts, Mary Christmas reminded me of Monique, our blue-eyed, blonde neighbor. My father often held the ladder in place as she climbed the apple tree to collect fruit. Mother always had lots of apple pies in the house.

I was still confused about Mrs. Claus. "I thought she was older," I said to Rudolph.

"Oh no; in keeping with the Kringle family tradition, Santa married his much-younger cousin; but the publicity department thought it was bad for his image."

I was feeling warmer and I asked about the source of the heat.

"From the heat well in the center plaza. It lets heat from deep underground rise and it keeps the temperature in the village at seventy-five degrees year round. Unfortunately, it's a blessing and a curse for us," explained Rudolph.

"How so?"

"The dark elves use it to come to the surface; they rampage through the village, and go back to the underworld again. They do it every Friday, at the dead hour."

"At the dead hour?"

"Yes, Peter. The dead hour is half an hour before and half an hour after midnight. Good spirits roam in the first half-hour and bad ones in the second. This year we have already lost twenty percent of the packages, plus the food, wine, and beer they consume during the half hour past midnight. We can't do anything about it."

"Yeah, yeah, no violence at 'Santa's, Inc.,'" I said.

"That's right, young man, only loving, lots of loving here," said Mrs. Claus. "How old are you, by the way?"

"Eight, but going on nine in ten months."

"Uhmmm," she said.

* * * * *

Santa was in his rocking chair on the porch when we saw him the first time. We sat on the floor in front of him and soon we were laughing at his life stories from all over the world.

"Long ago in New Guinea," he said, "the daughter of a tribal chief almost caught my foot in a snare before I hightailed it out of there, when I realized how big the iron kettle she wanted for Christmas was."

I asked what he was doing with the locksets on a table by his side.

"Learning to pick them," he said. "I'm tired of being stuck in chimneys."

The rest of the week we helped the light elves with packaging, organizing, making labels, and repairing broken toys. We ate in the cafeteria where we chatted with Santa every night, seated by the table with the chocolate malts and the bourbon bonbons. It was Santa's favorite place where he was surrounded by every dessert imaginable and then some.

When Friday came around, everyone changed. Santa lost his appetite, and my friends and I were the only ones eating. At thirty minutes before midnight, Santa and Mary went to their room to pray, and all the light elves enclosed themselves in their hostels. The reindeer had been secured in the stable.

However, I went with my friends to spy on the dark elves. We hid on the roof behind chimneys and waited.

At the stroke of midnight on the town's clock, a couple dozen humanoid creatures crawled out of the well, scuttling and screaming like monkeys. They had hairy heads and legs but clean green torsos, pointed ears, bulky eyes, no forehead, and serrated, deformed teeth. Their spines protruded from the base of their heads to their tailbones, which extended a foot out of the sacrum and ended in a curved scorpion claw.

They assaulted the cafeteria, picking up food with their knotty fingers, but mostly by shooting their tongues up to three feet out of their mouths and grabbing food with the sticky end.

In the half hour past twelve, they vandalized the dining area and gift-wrapping department. They jumped frantically from place to place as if aware of their time limitation. At the end of the allotted time, they tripped over each other in a desperate run back to the well, while greedily hoarding muffins and chocolates in their hands and mouths. They struggled, trying to enter all at once; however, one of them could not make it on time and seemed to faint, inches from the well, where he lay briefly before dematerializing in a milky energy puff.

The cleaning and reorganizing took most of Saturday morning. For the next few days, things were back to normal. But having observed the dark elves' behavior, we had a plan.

Santa came to ask what we could do. He calmed himself by eating chocolate.

"We will have our weapons ready next Friday," I said.

"Oh nooo, none of that, no weapons in here," lamented Santa.

"Our weapon is food; you don't have to worry, Santa."

* * * * *

That afternoon, while at work in the toyshop, Bonnie asked me "Why didn't you tell Santa about our other weapons?"

"What you don't know doesn't hurt you," I said.

The next few days, we took rides around town on the reindeer' backs; however, we did not neglect our other assigned duties. Friday came around again and we ordered the cooks to make a few hundred additional, extra-large moist chocolate muffins, powdered with sugar and nuts.

"Stash the muffins and bonbons on the roof as soon as they are ready," I told Bernie.

"Yes, Peter. We all have been piling them up there."

"Bonnie, you climb the clock tower and slow the hands by five minutes. When the dark elves crawl out at the first strike of the bell, it will be five minutes past twelve, but they won't know it," I said.

With the eleven-thirty mandatory curfew, the village became a ghost town. The first gong echoed; the creatures appeared and began their pillaging. At twelve twenty they scrambled back to the well. Most, if not all of them, were inebriated, their bellies distended owing to the food orgy.

"My mom said that gluttony is a deadly sin," I said and gave the order. From the roof we bombarded them with muffins. The size of the falling muffins made them unable to resist the temptation and they went berserk trading their loot for the new, more succulent ones.

Unaware of their tardiness until they felt sluggish, they became confused; they looked at the clock, and then at us.

Malignant but not stupid, they realized what was going on, and scrambled to reach the well. Our time had come. Out came our slingshots and we used the bonbons we had piled on the roof as projectiles. It was like shooting empty cans by the river.

We hit them everywhere; their tailbones appeared to be particularly sensitive, making them even groggier. The delicious bonbons tempted them again, and even in the midst of their panic, they attempted to gulp some of them. None returned to their underground lair in time. We watched them fall, puff, and vanish.

* * * * *

"Santa couldn't believe you got rid of them with only extra food," said Rudolph on the flight home.

"To tell the truth, the big glass marbles we put inside the bonbons helped to knock them down," said Bernard. "But don't tell him."

"I won't. Santa would not condone such action. He certainly would fire me."

We had a wonderful Christmas that year. Every child on each side of the river got gifts. There were so many toys to distribute that Mrs. Claus came around to help, but she may have been a little clumsy with her magic and awoke many of the dads in the area. Strangely, none of the moms heard anything. The morning after, I heard Mom and a friend talking about empty bottles of wine and two glasses they found in their respective living rooms.

As we grew up, we kept our adventure secret from the grownups. Then Bernard and I noticed that the older kids did not talk about it anymore. One day, Bobby and Bonnie made fun of Bernie and me for talking about Santa.

"We are too old to keep inventing such stories," said Bonnie.

* * * * *

Yesterday Bernard graduated from junior high, a year ahead of me. In a moment of quiet during the celebration with our families, Bernie and I began to talk.

"It would be nice if Rudolph were around and we could take a ride above the school," I said.

Bernard seemed puzzled.

"Who?"

THE NEW BICYCLE
by Isabel A. Worden-Klym

Christmas day dawned.
The bright shining snow
held promise.

Next to the tree
stood a red bicycle
ready to ride.

I ripped through
all the presents
and then went outside

with my prize.
It didn't matter
that I couldn't ride.

Three days later
I no longer fell
into the protective snow.

I could ride
to the end of the block
and back home,

a personal victory.
I taught myself
to stay upright.

Christmas night I slept,
my head full
of speeding wheels.

THE BOX
by Bill Lamperes

About the Author

Bill Lamperes grew up in Chicago and spoke Greek and German in his home. After spending thirty years as an educator in Colorado, he moved to Arizona and invented an alternative school based on the ideas in his book, *Making Change Happen: Shared Vision, No Limits*.

After retiring a second time, Bill began writing novels. His first, *Bar Exam: Tavern Tales and Reflections,* invites readers to listen to conversations ordinary people share about life, love and fate. *Depositions*, his second novel, is an intriguing murder mystery written with the spirit of a man who died in 1996. *The Attendant* is a romantic mystery involving a scam artist and a clairvoyant who pursues him from New York to the Greek Islands. His fourth novel, *Voices*, is an action-packed pursuit of a hit-and-run driver that takes readers into the paranormal world of ghostly messages. Bill currently lives in Glendale, Arizona.

Growing up, I realized Christmas at my house was very different than the holiday my friends celebrated. Other kids bragged about the loot Santa left under the tree and flaunted the newest clothing styles at school. Their lunchboxes overflowed with candy and other goodies discovered in the stockings hung by the fireplace. We had no fireplace and the concept of receiving sweets in an oversized stocking made my father scorn in broken English, "Socks are for wearing… not filled with food. What's the matter with Americans?"

My European parents had immigrated to this country and had worked hard to make their three children's lives better. They had no formal schooling, could barely read and spoke English with a heavy accent. My father, a struggling barber, whose trade barely paid the bills, required Mother to stay home and take care of the family. His philosophy was simple: "No good ever come from woman working and neglecting babies." The couple sacrificed, scrimped and saved for our future, not theirs. To reduce spending, Mother employed such measures as laundering Father's barber towels at night in an old wringer-washer. She'd then hang them to dry on a clothesline that snaked through our already tight living quarters.

The five of us inhabited a small apartment above the barbershop. It consisted of two tiny bedrooms, a small living room, a kitchen and one bathroom. Mother spent most of the day cooking, cleaning and keeping her rambunctious children quiet so we wouldn't disturb Father's customers sitting directly below the apartment. Whenever my father needed help, he'd bang on the heat pipes with a hammer as a signal for one of us to come downstairs and sweep up the hair that had accumulated around his barber chair.

During the Christmas season, my parents tried to be sensitive to our fragile emotional needs. They successfully ignored the excessive consumption surrounding us by creating a special family celebration of our own. Mother placed homemade candles throughout our apartment and tacked a plastic wreath from a garage sale on the front door. Because of space limitations, she set a two-foot, artificial Christmas tree on the coffee table in the living room. We decorated it with tinsel and various safely stored homemade ornaments lovingly fashioned in previous years. The feeble, pathetic-looking symbol of the season hardly supported the additional weight of its trimmings, but we were always proud of it.

With the tree decorated, Mother placed an old bed sheet around its base and the Christmas season officially began. As the days grew closer to December 25th, we put small, handcrafted gifts under the tree. The best part was the care we took in wrapping each box, as if the covering itself, and not the present, expressed our affection. Selected pictures from the Sunday comics or hand drawn designs on pieces of brown grocery bags provided the desired personal touch to our gifts. My parents insisted the Magi's unselfish act of devotion for baby Jesus, and not the Santa Claus myth, was the true source of the gift giving tradition. By personalizing special gifts for each other, we could genuinely share the meaning of love.

On Christmas morning, the family gathered in the living room and participated in the gift opening ritual relived year after year. One by one, we took turns searching the base of the tree for individual packages. Each of us paused to admire and fawn over the wrapping paper, vigorously shaking the box and guessing its contents. Gushes of genuine appreciation replaced squeals of laughter as the open containers revealed a crocheted scarf, a colored picture, a silver dollar, a pair of socks or some recycled toy from a previous birthday. It was such a hokey tradition, but we accepted our parents' wishes and now, as adults, fondly cherish the memory.

It wasn't until I became less self-centered and more observant that I realized one of Mother's presents was never opened in front of the family. It was a small box, wrapped in elegant silver paper, held together by a small piece of tape and surrounded by a thin strand of green ribbon. Year after year, the same box appeared under the tree, eventually showing signs of age. The box, with Mother's name on it, was always the last remaining present. By the time she picked it up, most of us had opened our gifts and lost interest in the event. Mother would notice our restless behavior and say, "Okay, children, now it's time to eat! I'll open this one later." We'd shout in unison and head for the kitchen immediately, while Mother's box would conveniently disappear.

For a European family, serving and consuming lots of good food was the most loving present. Christmas brunch, the one time a year my parents splurged, was incomparable to any other meal we ever shared. It consisted of several egg dishes, mounds of grilled potatoes, a variety of sausages, homemade cinnamon rolls and freshly-squeezed orange juice. On Christmas morning, we enjoyed food as if we were royalty. After breakfast the dishes were washed and we children drifted off to play. Father, with trousers unbuttoned, found his easy chair and became engrossed in a televised football game. With a sense of routine returning to the apartment, Mother, like clockwork, disappeared into the bedroom and took her traditional "Christmas nap." I had always thought Christmas preparations made her tired until once, inadvertently, I walked into the bedroom and found her softly crying. I just figured she felt bad because they couldn't afford to buy us more toys. How naïve I was as an adolescent.

As I grew older, watching Mother's Christmas behavior became an object of curiosity. My detective mind concluded her Christmas nap was an excuse to enjoy a good cry. Weeping in public was never an option for such a strong-willed woman. The mystery of the unopened silver box also bothered me, but I never had the nerve to ask about it. As the years passed, I often teased my aging mother about her special gift. However, she'd always ignore my inquisitiveness, slip the box into her apron, and utter those magic words, "Time to eat!" Mama's culinary delights always diverted our attention and kept the secret of her box safe for another year.

As time passed, we kids all graduated, landed good jobs, married and had children of our own. My brother became a well-known hairstylist, and my sister worked as a marketing consultant. I became a teacher and writer. My parents' dream to ensure our success had been realized. The new families created modern-day Christmas traditions, and Mother's box was all but forgotten.

Our father's sudden death in August, followed by Mother's passing in October, stunned us, wrenching each of our hearts with an emotional void. In an attempt to salvage cherished memories and celebrate our parents' lives, I invited my brother and sister to spend an old-fashioned, "traditional" Christmas morning with me. I wanted to recreate the ritual, the ceremonial customs that had held our family together throughout our youth.

When my parents died, I temporarily stored all their belongings in my basement. In preparation for our unique Christmas celebration, I rummaged through the containers and wrapped various sentimental items so my siblings could open their gifts on Christmas morning. One carton marked "Christmas" included treasured holiday decorations Mother had saved from the past. Respectfully, I hung these items in prominent places on my twelve-foot-tall, live tree. To my delight, I also found Mother's silver box. Now old and dusty, it looked like it had been opened and resealed. I shook it like a kid and still couldn't determine its contents. My discovery, I surmised, would offer my sister and brother an exceptional treat—to see Mother's box under my tree, open it together and finally discover an answer to her mystery.

The nostalgic Christmas morning was a huge success. Laughter and tears filled the room as one "gift" after another evoked fond recollections and hilarious stories. After all the personal items had been unwrapped, I announced we had one final present to open. I retrieved the silver package with its matted green bow from behind the tree and held it in my hands like a precious gem. Everyone immediately recognized Mother's box.

Gently, almost reverently, I removed the ribbon and the dried piece of tape that almost fell off. Once free of its fragile restraints, I lightly slipped off the lid. As I peered into the box, I saw a layer of black soil under a folded, handwritten note. The penciled German words were faded and difficult to interpret, but with the help of an Internet translation program, the message revealed our Mother's long-guarded secret. We read it together.

> *Susse Liebe (Sweet Love), As our oldest daughter, I send you to America to marry a man you do not know or love. He send us money... so we keep our farm. I know you will someday love him and be happy, but whenever you get lonely, open this box... look inside... feel... smell... remember your homeland... and us. Always know your sacrifice saved our home... I am proud of you... Love, Your Papa.*

Astonished and overwhelmed, the three of us sat in silence as tears of sadness streamed down our cheeks. None of us had ever known Mother was a war bride and the marriage to Father was a financial arrangement, not a union of love. She never told us the story, never complained about life, and never saw her family again. Stoically, Mother accepted her fate, married Father and privately mourned—once a year, at Christmas, when she opened the silver box and cried.

OTHER BOOKS BY OUR AUTHORS

All the following books can be purchased from Dog-Eared Pages Used Books, Phoenix, Arizona.

Bill Lamperes:

- *Making Change Happen: Shared Vision, No Limits.* Nonfiction about how we turned an alternative school around. Published 2005 by Scarecrow Education. Available at rowmaneducation.com.
- *Bar Exam: Tavern Tales and Reflections.* Fascinating dialogue of ordinary people at the Benbow Tavern. Published July, 2008. Available at Borders, Benbow Inn in Garberville, California, and select book stores; online at IUniverse and Amazon.
- *Depositions,* co authored by **Leon Palles**. Twisting tale of suspense and mystery. Published December, 2008. Available at Borders and select book stores; online at IUniverse and Amazon.
- *The Attendant.* Story of a man who scammed the system and got away with it, or so he thought. Published July, 2010. Available at Borders and select book stores; online at IUniverse and Amazon.

Lesley Sudders writing as Les Brierfield:

- *The Brodick Follies.* Mystery novel. Harry Brodick, illegal arms dealer and former mercenary soldier, dies in a Colorado ski resort town. Was he murdered by his wife, her lover, former enemies, or new associates? First volume in The Thunder Ridge Trilogy. Published September, 2009, by Strategic Book Publishing. Available at Barnes & Noble or directly from publisher; online from author at www.brierfieldbooks.com or Amazon; in digital format from Smashwords, http://tinyurl.com/brodickfollies

Eduardo Cerviño writing as Ed Brierfield:

- *In My Other Body.* Science fiction tale dealing with the synergy of the human race in parallel universes. Look for release in early 2011.
- *The Girl in the Basket.* Novel about the healing power of love. Look for release in early 2011.

Collaborations by Lesley Sudders and Eduardo Cerviño, writing as Les and Ed Brierfield:

- *Harry's Ghost.* Volume II in The Thunder Ridge Trilogy. Harry Brodick's restless ghost returns to haunt and taunt those he thought responsible for his death. But in the end, does he seek revenge, or redemption? Available in digital format from Smashwords, http://tinyurl.com/harrysghost
- *The Cult of Iona.* Volume III in The Thunder Ridge Trilogy. A cursed Scottish clan moves to Thunder Ridge to continue its evil practices. The clan mistress rules through murder, sorcery and seduction, but may have found her match in Harry Brodick and other spirits. Look for release in early 2011.
- *Opium Den.* Collection of magic realism short stories that explores emotions from anger and fear to tender love, from wonder to awful truths, from kindness to brutality. Available in digital format from Smashwords, http://tinyurl.com/opiumanthology

Melanie Tighe writing as Anna Questerly:

- Look for Melanie's debut novel, *The Minstrel's Tale*, for children ages ten and up, to be released May 2, 2011.

Jerry's Writers Group:

- *The Second Annual Holiday Anthology.* Collection of holiday stories and poetry for the 2009 holiday season. Published October, 2009. Available online at Amazon.